June 23, 98

Dear Bob:

When you are traveling to Israel this year, undoubtedly you will bring back lasting memories.

Each person experiences this Holy Land in a different way.

When I first read some chapters of this book I could not connect until I experienced these holy places myself.

I am certain you will meet God in new ways not seen before when visiting this land.

May this book stimulate you for this exciting adventure.

Your friend
Robert

MEETING GOD IN HOLY PLACES

A Devotional Journey

F. LaGard Smith

illustrated by GLENDA RAE

HARVEST HOUSE PUBLISHERS
Eugene, Oregon 97402

Cover illustration by Glenda Rae
Cover by Garborg Design Works, Minneapolis, Minnesota

MEETING GOD IN HOLY PLACES
Copyright © 1997 by F. LaGard Smith
Published by Harvest House Publishers
Eugene, Oregon 97402

Library of Congress Cataloging-in-Publicaation Data

Smith, F. LaGard (Frank LaGard), 1944-
    Meeting God in holy places / F. LaGard Smith.
        p.   cm.
    ISBN 1-56507-521-8
    1. Palestine—Description and travel. 2. Smith, F. LaGard (Frank LaGard),
1944-   —Journeys—Palestine. 3. Meditations. 4. Christian shrines—Palestine—Meditations.
I. Title.
DS107.5.S64   1997
220.9'1—dc21   97-5438
                                                                                         CIP

Printed in the United States of America.

97 98 99 00 01 02 / DH / 10 9 8 7 6 5 4 3 2 1

Dedication

Dedicated to Ben and Jane Batey,

who gave me Ruth,

and in whose lives

holy places are always close at hand.

Appreciation

To my friend and brother, Joseph Shulam,

who has taught me most of what I know

about the holy places of Israel.

As a Jerusalem-raised, Messianic Jew,

Joseph knows both Israel and Scripture like few others—

and loves to share his special land

with enthusiasm and passion.

Thanks for the memories and the messages, Joseph.

This book comes from your heart as well as mine.

Contents

The Journey Begins . . .

"Israel was

holy to the LORD."

JEREMIAH 2:3

In Holy Places

The last time we met, in *Meeting God in Quiet Places*, we walked together through the quaint villages and green hills of the Cotswolds in the English countryside. We talked about badgers and bunnies, seasons and sunsets, gargoyles and grave-stones. Even sheep droppings!

It was a quiet, meditative walk with God through the beauty of nature which he created. Everywhere we looked in nature, God gave us a parable. Nature itself is the Great Parable, telling us about the God who made us and loves us.

This time we will walk together in the land of Israel, redis-covering the holy places where God interacted with his chosen people in a special way. I say "holy places," knowing that it is not the places themselves that are holy, but the recorded presence of God in those places that has made them so.

We will often find ourselves in Jerusalem, the City of David, at sites that hold special meaning because of their association with biblical events—the pools of Siloam and Bethesda, where Jesus performed at least two of his many miracles of healing; the Via

Dolorosa (or Way of Sorrows), on which Jesus walked to his cruci-fixion; and the tomb where Jesus is thought to have lain. And we will walk up the Mount of Olives and stop to meditate in the quiet Garden of Gethsemane.

Jerusalem is a city of contrasts and conflict, of deep faith and religious division. Even now, centuries removed from the time of Christ, you can almost see Jesus weeping over it, crying once again, "O Jerusalem, Jerusalem . . . how often I have longed to gather your children together, as a hen gathers her chicks under her wings, but you were not willing."

Yet Jerusalem was always special to God. It was Jerusalem where God chose to have Solomon build the temple. Jerusalem, where Jesus made his triumphal entry on the foal of a donkey. Jerusalem, where the Good News would first be preached by the apostles. No wonder we look forward to *the heavenly Jerusalem!*

Beyond Jerusalem, we will visit many other places where Jesus walked, including the Sea of Galilee, center of Jesus' ministry and miracles. We will eat St. Peter's fish along the shore and look out over wind-whipped whitecaps that remind us of the occasion when Jesus said to the storm and the sea, "Quiet! Be still!" And of the time when Jesus walked on the water, and Peter launched out to do the same, but lost faith and began to sink.

A visit to Israel is like seeing the Bible in technicolor. All the familiar Bible stories we've heard and read from our youth dra-matically jump off the page and come to life! Stand on the Mount of Beatitudes on a lovely spring day, and you're surrounded on every side by the very "lilies of the field" and "birds of the air" of which Jesus spoke. Why, indeed, should we worry? "Are you not much more valuable than they?"

In our moments together in the holy land, we will be not just *tourists* but *pilgrims*. Forget the icons dripping with gold at the Church of the Nativity in Bethlehem. Who can know the *exact* spot where Jesus was born? The point is that, somewhere in that lowly village south of Jerusalem, God surprised us by coming into our world so that we might enter into his. That is the incredible impact of a visit to Israel.

As you walk away from Bethlehem, or Gethsemane, or the Jordan River, your life will never again be the same. You've walked on "holy ground." You've touched and been touched. You've seen the face of God more clearly than ever before.

I've been to Israel several times now—on my own, in small groups, and most recently with my wife, Ruth. (In *Meeting God in Quiet Places*, I walked in solitude. Since then God has given me a companion to walk by my side. After all these years, he *is* a God of surprises!)

This time I want to take you with me. If you've never been to these "holy places" before, take a seat next to the window and feast your eyes on the passing terrain. Israel is beautiful, fascinating, and vibrant. But, most of all, it is the land where God chose to reveal himself to us. As we travel back through the centuries, what we will discover is not just history, but *his story*—and thus ours.

If you've been to Israel before, perhaps you've missed something along the way. Each time I return, I discover something new. No, not simply another tourist attraction, but something deep within myself that is prompted by what I see: a new thought; a different perspective; a grander vision of who I can be as a servant of God.

So, whether it's your first time or a return visit, come along on this spiritual pilgrimage. You too might well discover some hidden holy places within your own heart.

As before, our journey together will be enhanced by the beauty and warmth of Glenda Rae's lovely pencil sketches. No other artist has ever captured in quite the same way the softness of Israel's often harshly depicted motifs. Looking through her eyes of faith, we come to see both the land and its people in a way we've never seen them before.

Sight and insight. These are the objects of our journey. And where better to find them than when we meet God in holy places of his own choosing?

Chapter One

"Tomorrow the LORD

will do amazing things

among you."

JOSHUA 3:5

Surprise

As I drove toward Bethlehem, my natural curiosity was begging to know every detail. What would it have been like for Joseph and Mary as they approached Bethlehem 20 centuries ago? Was the five-mile stretch of road from Jerusalem as bustling as it is today? What did they see? What did they hear? Were they too tired from their long journey to think anything at all, or were they talking excitedly about getting settled in and having Mary's baby?

Today, travelers wind their way slowly through a maddening throng of cars with honking horns, smoky tour buses, and military vehicles. Ironically, most of the people on this road today probably would not even be here had it not been for Joseph and Mary coming to this unlikely spot.

In truth, the road might have seemed just as crowded to Joseph and Mary. At the time of their journey, Bethlehem was a stopover for commercial caravaners on their way from Jerusalem south to Hebron. And, of course, the reason for their traveling all the way down from Nazareth in the north was the tax census requiring each person to be enrolled in his own city.

That meant a host of David's descendants coming into Bethlehem, the city of David's birth. Smoky buses and honking horns may barely rival the dust kicked up by the camel trains and the noise of donkeys braying along the way.

As you approach the town, what first catches your eye are all the terraced olive groves, which march up the dry hills like steps leading to a temple. And then, suddenly, there it is: Bethlehem, the ancient "House of Bread"—clinging to a ridge as if clinging to history itself. "O, little town of Bethlehem, how still we see thee lie!"

But who could believe how different today's Bethlehem is from all those quaint-looking Bethlehems painted on the Christmas cards? What a surprise! Or, more honestly, what a *disappointment*. Could this really be the setting which God chose in which to bring such "joy to the world"?

As I arrive at the square, buses are disgorging scores of pilgrims who head immediately for the massive, fortresslike Church of the Nativity. Naturally, no one can be sure exactly where Jesus' birth occurred in Bethlehem, but you just know that, wherever the exact spot, it couldn't have been far away. That thought alone pierces through all the touristy glitz and fairly takes your breath away in anticipation.

My entrance into the ancient church is not made any easier by the height of the doorway, purposely made low, so it seems, to prevent any marauding Turks from riding their horses into the structure and desecrating it. Once inside the Greek Orthodox chapel, I discover a rather plain interior, but some beautiful mosaics in the original floor, and, of course, the mandatory icons. These particular icons seem to be absolutely dripping with gold. (There was incense, too, but myrrh was conspicuous by its absence.)

As you look around, it's hard not to be impressed by the antiquity of the building itself. (Not only is it the oldest church in Israel, but it is one of the oldest anywhere, having been constructed originally by Constantine and his mother, Helena, in A.D. 325.) But it's not some man-made structure I have come to see, but rather the grotto beneath the church, said to be the place of Jesus' birth. So I quickly leave the gilded icons and the throngs of pilgrims who are enraptured by them, and head directly for the grotto, taking the stairs which lead beneath the main altar.

Anyone expecting to see the manger scene as depicted in Bible story books and in classic art is in for yet another surprise. There is no inn, no wooden manger, no straw, and certainly no gentle animals looking on. Just more gaudiness, featuring a white, marble-lined niche in a cave wall, dimly lit by hanging lamps and accented by a blackened 14-point silver star.

Which is better? I wonder: Never having ever been to the site of Jesus' birth, yet somehow being able to visualize it in imaginative technicolor from the Scripture's own brief account, or being right there in Bethlehem, yet being robbed of one's lifetime collage of manger-scene images by an overly embellished representation of the blessed event?

Or, indeed, have there always been surprises surrounding Jesus' birth? Were you surprised, for example, when you first learned that December 25 was an unlikely date for the first "Christmas"—that it most likely took place in the spring, when the hills would be covered with grass for the grazing of the sheep? Is it surprising, even now, not to know exactly how many wise men came to pay homage to the baby Jesus? (The traditional "three" is merely surmised from the three gifts which were brought.) Or that the wise men were never part of the manger scene in the first place, arriving probably some six months after Jesus' birth, not at a manger, but at "the house" where Joseph and Mary were more securely living by that time?

If you are surprised by those details, imagine King Herod's surprise when the magi appeared and inquired of Jesus' whereabouts. Unfamiliar with Micah's prophecy regarding Bethlehem being the Messiah's birthplace, he could never have expected that some other "king" would be born in his jurisdiction, especially the King of kings! To Herod, that thought was not just surprising but threatening. For someone so hopelessly unacquainted with the God of surprises as he was, a sense of joy would have been the last thing ever to cross his mind.

By contrast, when the shepherds in the field were surprised by the appearances of the angel and the heavenly host, their initial terror quickly turned to joy. Just as the angel had said, they found the baby "wrapped in cloths and lying in a manger." For simple men with open hearts, it was a process of surprise, shock, fear, disbelief, hope, trust, confirmation, and, finally, indescribable joy! Joy at seeing the Christ child. Joy at having been singled out for the unique honor of being present at the very moment in history when God came near. Joy at having witnessed the one birth that gives meaning to all other births.

Why lowly shepherds? Why humble Bethlehem? Why an obscure virgin girl from Nazareth? If you and I had written the story line, would it have been anything like the divine drama? Surely, that's what God's surprises are all about—grabbing our attention, altering our realities, turning our world and our values and our preconceptions upside down! Just when we think we have God in a box, he springs out in surprise and sends us reeling! With God, almost nothing is as it seems.

Have you ever been surprised by joy?

You can bet that Abraham and Sarah were surprised by joy, not unlike many couples today who give up on having the baby they want, only to discover that God has worked a marvelous miracle in the hopeful womb.

And what about Hannah, whose joy in the surprise of answered prayer is echoed generation after generation whenever God takes the seemingly impossible and makes it possible?

Of course, no one was more surprised than Mary herself, and then Joseph, when the impending birth was first announced by the angel. For Joseph and Mary, "surprised" was hardly the word; more likely "astonished!" What could possibly be more surprising than a virgin becoming pregnant! As with the shepherds, it must have been a process of surprise, shock, fear, disbelief, hope, trust, and then—*disappointment!* "Could it really be," Mary must have asked herself, "that the Messiah will be born tonight in this dark, smelly pit in the earth?" Yet when she heard those first cries of divine life wrapped in human flesh, any thought of disappointment must surely have turned into immeasurable peace and joy!

Could all the world's artistry put together have made the scene that wondrous night more beautiful? Or all the marble or silver stars crafted by human hand? The surprising thing about joy is that it is almost always a surprise! It's almost never the scene we might expect.

What do we learn from the unlikely circumstances of Jesus' birth, but that our God is a God of surprises. How he delights in bringing us unexpected joy! How many times have we seen God most clearly in the middle of a crisis? How many times have we discovered the *miraculous* in the midst of the *mundane*? Somehow you just know that, when God has a really special gift in mind for us, he'll wrap it in such a way that we would never guess what's inside the package.

When you think about it, it shouldn't be all that surprising. God's greatest gift of all—greater even than the particular circumstances of Jesus' birth—was the incarnation. Whoever could have guessed? The Son of God himself was wrapped in ordinary human flesh so that you and I, in turn, might become extraordinary!

With that thought, it hardly matters that a shrine meant to celebrate the birth of Jesus all too easily disappoints us. By what right would anyone ever expect that Jesus' miraculous appearance could adequately be captured by any human effort? Not all the gold and burning tapers and treasured icons in the world could ever hope to capture the essence of something as surprisingly unworldly as Jesus' birth.

But then, that's what so fun about being one of God's children: Just when we least expect it, God surprises us with pearls of joy gift-wrapped in plain brown paper!

Chapter Two

"Where, O grave,

is your destruction?"

HOSEA 13:14

Bonding

Every fiber of my being recoiled at the sight. From the heady mixture of Crusader and Byzantine styles, to the pretentious religious trappings, to the notorious jurisdictional infighting among the five sects which maintain the shrine, I was anything but comfortable as I gazed about the Church of the Holy Sepulchre. If others were deeply moved, I was only offended.

"Is this how Jesus felt when he threw the moneychangers out of the temple?" I wondered.

Not, of course, that I hadn't expected to see exactly what I saw. (Or perhaps I saw only what I had *expected* to see.) But in that moment I gained a new respect for the Jews, who dare not set foot on Temple Mount lest they inadvertently tread on "holy ground." If, as claimed, the Church of the Holy Sepulchre is the actual site of Jesus' crucifixion and burial, then the area surely deserves more respect—perhaps a park, with nothing more than an austere viewing stand and a strictly enforced quiet zone.

Yet I must admit that I had not been dragged there against my will. I was led to the shrine by the same curiosity which has driven millions of pilgrims and tourists there over the centuries in the hope of somehow "touching" the central cornerstones of Christian faith: the cross and the tomb.

Maybe that's the very reason I was offended. If I had come to "touch" and to "be touched," the shrine itself was keeping that from happening. Far from venerating the site, the holy hoopla and religious regalia got in the way of the moving spiritual experience for which I longed.

But suddenly it happened. Just as I was about to mentally run screaming out of the church in a desperate flight from its desecration, our guide, Joseph, pulled us away from the lavishly decorated holy sepulchre, with all its ritual smells and bells. In a hushed tone, Joseph suggested that we walk behind the "official tomb" to a cavelike tomb which lacked pomp and circumstance, but which likely would have been the kind of carved-out sepulchre in which Jesus was buried.

One by one our little band squeezed into the darkened tomb, illuminated only by a single match which Joseph had lit. Once inside, the flame flickered, then died. Wrapped in total darkness, all conversation ceased as each one of us receded into our own private thoughts.

I remember thinking how damp and musty it smelled. How cold and foreboding it felt. How cramped and claustrophobic. I could only begin to imagine how trapped I would have felt if a stone had been rolled across the entrance.

There in the darkness of the tomb, two thoughts rushed to my mind in rapid succession with a force I couldn't begin to describe: Incredibly, the Lord of heaven and earth was actually buried in such a place. . . .

And, who knows, perhaps this *very* place!

Never have I felt closer to the Person of Jesus. It's one thing to read about his life and death, and even to put one's complete faith in him. It's another thing altogether to feel his presence so closely and intimately—as if he were lying there, wrapped in a linen burial cloth, right next to you.

"Blessed are those who have not seen and yet have believed," Jesus said to Thomas, who, having seen Jesus' wounds, joyously proclaimed his faith in the resurrected Lord. "Blessed, too," I thought to myself, "are those who *have* seen . . . if only in some special way like this."

Do you know what it is like to be swallowed up in the darkness of despair? Or to be slowly suffocating in a dead-end job? Or, perhaps, trapped in a lifeless marriage? God in human flesh allowed himself to be trapped in the suffocating darkness of a cold, musty tomb, as if to say: "Wherever you are, I'll be with you. I've been there before."

Deeply moved by Jesus' "presence" in the tomb, it occurred to me that it is usually an *empty* tomb we celebrate as believers. The tomb which we prefer to envision has the stone rolled away. It is a tomb of resurrection and rejoicing. And why not? Our Savior is a risen Lord!

But, in between his cruel crucifixion and glorious resurrection, perhaps we have missed something important about Jesus' burial—indeed, about our own burial. What else could Paul possibly be trying to tell us? "We were therefore buried with him through baptism into death in order that, just as Christ was raised from the dead through the glory of the Father, we too may live a new life."

It's a case of first things first. Before the stone can be rolled away from our own spiritual tombs, we must first be buried with Christ. If we want to be identified with Christ in *life*, we must first identify with Christ in *death*. It's no use rushing to the empty tomb if along the way we have failed to grasp what it means to be buried with Christ. "Don't you know that all of us who were baptized into Christ Jesus were baptized into his death?"

Beyond the symbolism of baptism is the very real need we have for identification. Just as God identifies with us in all the many ways in which we are enshrouded in darkness, so too we must somehow identify with him in his entombment. Call it bonding. The joy which comes in the morning can only be fully appreciated by those who have died to the world and allowed their former selves to be buried in Christ's own tomb.

Resurrection always requires a burial.

One of the most intriguing Old Testament stories is about a man of God who is sent on a mission to Bethel to warn an idolatrous King Jeroboam of pending punishment. Mission accomplished, the man of God is invited to stay and have lunch with the king. But the man of God refuses, saying that he has been specifically instructed to neither eat, drink, nor return by the way which he had come. So he refuses the king's hospitality and goes on his way.

For reasons undisclosed, an older prophet intercepts the man of God and lies to him, saying that an angel of the Lord has revealed a special counterorder. Acting in good faith on that information, the man of God is persuaded to go and eat with the older prophet; but, on his return journey, the man of God is killed by a lion! (The seeming unfairness of that outcome is softened in a later passage where the memory of the man of God—rather much like the disobedient Moses—is singled out for honor.)

What happens next is even more intriguing. When the older prophet is told about the man of God's death, he hurries to the scene, takes the man's body, and buries it in his own tomb—distraught and weeping because of his own act of deception. Then, to his sons, the older prophet says, "When I die, bury me in the grave where the man of God is buried; lay my bones beside his bones . . . for the message he declared . . . will certainly come true."

One might be excused for dismissing the passage as a nice piece of ancient literature with an interesting twist in the story line. But I think the prophet was onto something when he insisted upon being buried, bone to bone, with the man of God.

When we, like him, are buried "bone to bone with the Son of God," we thereby share in his mission and in the truth of his message. And in that there is life!

Just when we think that, for whatever reason, our lives are ebbing away into total despair—helpless and hopeless—it's time to join Jesus in his tomb and quietly lie beside him, "bone to bone." For in his bones there is life.

What was it that God said to Ezekiel in his vision of the dry bones? "I will attach tendons to you and make flesh come upon you and cover you with skin; I will put breath in you, and you will come to life. Then you will know that I am the LORD."

The picture God gives us is not one of shrouds and sepulchres, nor death and decay. It's just the opposite. Praise God, it's the opposite!

It's not a *tomb* he's describing, but a *womb*!

And somehow we all sensed this at the same time. In the

quiet, dark stillness of the Jerusalem tomb, we began to softly sing Henry Lyte's prayerful hymn:

> Abide with me: fast falls the eventide;
> The darkness deepens: Lord, with me abide!
> When other helpers fail and comforts flee,
> Help of the helpless, O abide with me!
>
> Swift to its close ebbs out life's little day;
> Earth's joys grow dim, its glories pass away;
> Change and decay in all around I see;
> O Thou who changest not, abide with me!
>
> I fear no foe with Thee at hand to bless;
> Ills have no weight, and tears no bitterness;
> Where is death's sting? Where, grave, thy victory?
> I triumph still, if Thou abide with me!
>
> Hold Thou Thy cross before my closing eyes;
> Shine through the gloom, and point me to the skies;
> Heav'n's morning breaks, and earth's vain shadows flee;
> In life, in death, O Lord, abide with me!

And having sung a hymn, we went out . . . bone to bone with Jesus forever.

Chapter Three

"God so loved the world

that he gave his

one and only Son."

John 3:16

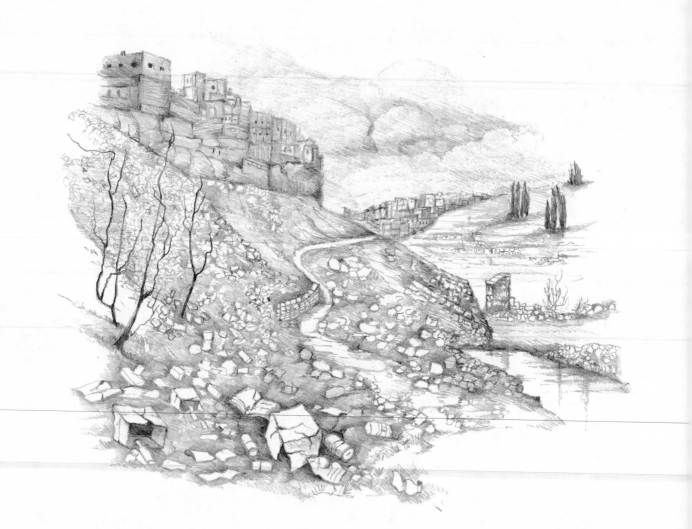

Providence

ou'd have to know the whole crew—Max, Stanley, Rubel, Joseph, and myself—and just how different we all are in order to appreciate the friendly banter and good-natured barbs that we were poking at each other while driving around Israel together in a rented van. Anyone who *did* know us would undoubtedly say that we were an altogether interesting mix of personalities, egos, and even doctrinal outlooks. Yet here we were, happily bundled up together in the middle of a bitterly cold Israeli winter, careening from side to side as Max drove like a madman while Joseph was shouting directions from the rear of the van.

As we neared the Wadi-er-Rababi (better known to most readers of the Bible as the Valley of Gehenna), the shout came out, "Max, go to hell and turn left!" By that time we all knew what Joseph meant. Throughout the course of the week we had repeatedly crossed down through the valley which is biblically associated with hell. At that someone chimed in, "It'll be a cold day in hell before this bunch of guys ever find themselves in the same van!"

From what we could see in the arcticlike conditions, Gehenna, a precipitous ravine which begins near the Jaffa Gate and stretches around the west and south of the old city until it joins the Kidron Valley, didn't look all that inviting. Nor, it seemed, would it look much cheerier even in warmer weather. But had it been warmer, the imagery would have been far more appropriate. In fact, the hotter the better, since one can hardly think of hell without thinking of fire and heat. Although hell is referred to as a *lake* burning with fire, not a burning valley, anyone familiar with Scripture will know that the Valley of Gehenna is closely linked to two different kinds of fire, and hence the picture of hell.

In ancient Israel, the Valley of Hinnom (as Gehenna was then known) was notorious as the site for sacrifices to the pagan god Molech. Not just the ordinary sacrifices, mind you, but even *child* sacrifices. The sacrifice of a pigeon permitted the worshiper to pass through the first gate, a sacrificed goat through the second, and so on. But only the sacrifice of one's son or daughter permitted a man to pass through the seventh and last gate into the very presence of Molech.

In this horrendous pagan practice, the worshiper would kiss his child and then place the child in the red-hot arms of the idol, inside of which was a continually burning fire. To muffle the screams of the children who were "passing through the fire," onlookers would frenetically beat loud drums. In fact, Topheth, at the southeast end of the valley, takes its very name from the root word *toph*, meaning drum.

The evil of sacrificing one's own child is so unthinkable that God, speaking through the prophet Jeremiah, said, "They have built the high places of Topheth in the Valley of Ben Hinnom to burn their sons and daughters in the fire—something I did not command, *nor did it enter my mind.*"

I confess I am equally perplexed as to how such a practice could ever have entered the mind of man!

So great was God's wrath on this issue that he vowed severe punishment for this detestable practice. "The days are coming . . . when people will no longer call it Topheth or the Valley of Ben Hinnom, but the Valley of Slaughter, for they will bury the dead in Topheth until there is no more room."

That very prophecy was fulfilled when Josiah later destroyed the altars, broke apart the idol Molech, and, in an eye-for-eye fashion, burned the bones of the pagan priests and dumped them into the valley.

From that point onward Gehenna became a kind of garbage dump for Jerusalem. It is from this garbage-dump usage of the valley that we encounter the second fire to be associated with hell ("where their worm does not die, and the fire is not quenched," as Jesus put it). This fire was a perpetual smoldering, constantly fueled by refuse that was thrown onto the fire. To complete the picture, there is even Jesus' imagery of bodies being "thrown into hell," as if into the burning garbage dump where they are consumed by the fire.

Dante's *Inferno*, with its guided tour of hell and all the various levels of suffering, unspeakable pain, shrieking, and torture, has probably shaped our thinking of hell more than anything strictly biblical, apart from Scripture's sobering reference to "weeping and gnashing of teeth." But who could possibly miss Jesus' own references to hell as being a place of punishment, banishment, and destruction? "Do not be afraid of those who kill the body but cannot kill the soul," Jesus warned. "Rather, be afraid of the One who can destroy both soul and body in hell."

Eternal punishment. Eternal destruction. Eternal banishment from the presence of God. Hell is not a pretty picture, nor a subject of any comfort. Jokes about "cold days in hell" and "hell freezing over" belie the seriousness of a subject all too easily dismissed for more comforting "warm fuzzies."

More difficult yet is the hard question inevitably asked about how a loving God could permit such a place of punishment and destruction. The most logical answer to that question takes us full circle back to child sacrifice and why hell is an appropriate consequence of such human horror.

I'm not thinking here merely of those who laid their sons and daughters on the red-hot arms of Molech while the drums drowned out the children's terrified screams. Instead, I am thinking of the rather more disturbing story of God calling Abraham to sacrifice his son Isaac on an altar. Because of the surprise ending—when God stops Abraham at the last minute—we tend to forget the events leading up to the knife in Abraham's hand, poised to do that which we would quickly condemn the pagan for doing.

Abraham indicates in every way possible that he believes Isaac will somehow be spared (if only by being brought back to life); and certainly God never intended to let Abraham go through with the killing. It was a test of Abraham's trust and commitment to God. But if offering Isaac as a sacrifice was God's idea, then what am I to make of God's response to the child sacrifice of Molech worship: "*nor did it enter my mind*"?

What can that possibly mean but that God could never have imagined people whose sensitivities were so callous as to be untouched by the cries of pain of their own children? That, apparently, was the very reason God chose child sacrifice as the ultimate test of Abraham's faith. No other test would ask so much dependence upon God's providence. To his eternal credit, Abraham's faith did not disappoint. "God will provide," was Abraham's answer to Isaac when he asked his father about the sacrificial lamb. "And to this day," Moses wrote of that incident, "it is said, 'On the mountain of the LORD it will be provided.'"

What then does the story of Abraham and Isaac tell us about hell? Is it merely that those who misdirect their faith to pagan gods and literally offer their children as sacrifices are, unlike Abraham, deserving of hell? If so, are those who sacrifice their children on the altars of divorce and dual careers and abortion any less deserving? Is there no mercy, no hope, for sinners all—including you and me—whatever the grievous sins we may have committed?

As I viewed the barren, foreboding Valley of Gehenna with its dark history and scriptural associations with hell, I could not help but hear over and over the words of Abraham: "The LORD will provide." And from the bottom of Gehenna—from the very pit of hell, as it were—I could almost see the cross of Christ just beyond the valley on the hill of Jerusalem. And again came the refrain, "On the mountain of the LORD it will be provided."

Provided indeed! If hell is the natural and appropriate consequence for the detestability of sin, God in his mercy has provided a way of escape. But not without great cost: the sacrifice of God's own Son.

For the unlovable, God did the unspeakable.

And as Jesus cried out in agony, "My God, my God, why

have you forsaken me?" the drums of heaven beat so loudly that "the earth shook and the rocks split."

Hell is not centrally about torture and pain, fire and flames, but, as one is reminded by a drive through the garbage dump of Gehenna, about lives wasted and destroyed. It's about the burning stench of eternal spiritual death that will render meaningless any life that has been lived in open rebellion to God, that has refused to accept the mercy of God, and that has shown abject contempt for the only child sacrifice ever made necessary.

So, with Max at the wheel and Joseph yelling out directions, we drove recklessly through hell and lived to tell about it. As we left the valley and drove to higher ground, it wasn't the shameful sound of pagan drums that lingered, nor the fearful prospect of fire and brimstone for the unrepentant wicked. It was, instead, a distant view of the cross of Jesus just beyond Gehenna, together with a vision back through time of a euphoric Abraham shouting over and over, "God provides! God provides! Praise God that, for sinners all, he provides!"

Chapter Four

"One greater

than the temple

is here."

MATTHEW 12:6

Presence

There was no mistaking the importance of what I was about to see. Turning left up a small alleyway just off David Street, all of a sudden I was confronted by heavily armed police and airportlike security. Because of Passover week and a recent spate of terrorist bombings there was even more tension in the air than usual. But I was determined to see what, for Jews, was the most holy place in Israel: the Wailing Wall.

Officially the wall is known as the "Western Wall," buttressing as it does the western side of Temple Mount. Formerly the plaza rising above the Western Wall was the site of Herod the Great's temple, and before that Solomon's temple and its later, less grand replacement built by the returning exiles under Ezra's leadership.

Herod's temple was destroyed when the Roman army under Titus invaded Jerusalem in A.D. 70. Jesus had predicted the event some 40 years earlier when one of his disciples was raving about the magnificent structures on Temple Mount. Bringing him up shortly, Jesus said, "Do you see all these great buildings? Not one stone here will be left on another; every one will be thrown down." The rubble proving the truth of his prediction lies just behind the Western Wall to this very day.

When Herod renovated the second temple at the end of the first century before Christ, he shored up the temple plaza on all sides by massive walls, up to six stories high. Although only half that height is visible above ground level today, the Western Wall is still impressive, particularly the 165-foot portion known as the Wailing Wall.

At that point the wall towers over the paving stones where people from all over the world come to pray and to insert scribbled "prayer lists" into crevices in the wall. For more sheltered praying, there are two enclosed porticos adjacent to the exposed wall—the one on the left, for men only; the one on the right, for women and children.

Stepping curiously inside the left portico, I was mesmerized by the rhythmic swaying that accompanied the prayers being said. Old men and young alike were dressed in traditional black, from the Orthodox broad-brimmed hats down to their long black coats and pointed shoes. To the uninitiated, the prayers seemed to be set pieces, either read or memorized, but they were presented with obvious faith and fervency.

Because I myself was one of the many tourists at the wall that day, I could not help but feel like an intruder into what I knew that for others was sacred space. Back in the States, my students facetiously refer to the board where their grades are posted as "the wailing wall." Here at the foot of the real Wailing Wall, I could sense in a most profound way that much more was at stake than merely a set of bad grades.

Having nothing left of their holy temple, Jews have come to regard the Wailing Wall as the ultimate symbol of their very Jewishness. In these ancient stones lies their religious and national identity, their long history of persecution, their heritage of exile, and their hope for future redemption. No wonder they pray here. No wonder they weep. No wonder they wail.

From the days of Mordecai and Esther to the horrors of the Holocaust, Jews have experienced relentless rejection and loss. When the Persian King Xerxes ordered the death of all Jews within Persia, "there was great mourning among the Jews, with fasting, weeping and wailing." Even 2500 years later, the wailing has not stopped.

To understand the Jews' identity with the temple, and thus the importance of the Wailing Wall, one has to go all the way back to the original temple built by Solomon. In his dedicatory prayer, Solomon marveled at the Divine Presence within the walls which he had constructed: "But will God really dwell on earth? The heavens, even the highest heaven, cannot contain you. How much less this temple I have built!"

Out of all the world, the Jews had been God's chosen people. To the Jews alone had God miraculously appeared in the cloud and in the sea. To the Jews alone had come the promise of a land, and of a name, and of an everlasting kingdom. When the glory of the LORD filled the temple, God was literally present in the midst of his people!

Do you long to have the presence of God in your life? Have you ever experienced the kind of sudden, unexpected pain or loss that needs to know where God can be found at a moment's notice? Do you ever wish that you had a place where you could go and always know that God would be there to meet you?

In times of struggle and sorrow, do we not all share the sentiments of King Jehoshaphat, who said, "If calamity comes upon us, whether the sword of judgment, or plague or famine, we will stand in your presence before this temple that bears your Name and will cry out to you in our distress, and you will hear us and save us"?

For Jews, the temple and God's presence were one and the same. So when they prayed, they prayed toward the temple; and in praying toward the temple, they came into the presence of God.

Never was that connection more pointedly demonstrated than when Jonah, in the belly of the great fish, cried in despair: "When my life was ebbing away, I remembered you, LORD, and my prayer rose to you, to your holy temple." Even there, in the depths of the sea, and in the jaws of pending death, Jonah's desperate prayer for salvation was still directed to God's temple.

Wouldn't it be nice to have, like Jonah, a compass-heading for God? To know at all times and in all circumstances where he can be found? But without a temple, or some sacred place, or an exact location for his presence, how can one ever be certain that God is there, or that he is listening?

It was this precise problem which confronted the Jews when their disobedience as a nation led God to withhold his presence from them. Hadn't he warned them against turning to other gods? Hadn't he sent prophet after prophet to call them out of the temples of man-made idols where there was perhaps *presence* but not *power*?

Micah, for one, had brought the ominous message: "Therefore because of you, Zion will be plowed like a field, Jerusalem will become a heap of rubble, the temple hill a mound overgrown with thickets." And he might well have added, "When that happens, you will have nothing more glorious than a retaining wall toward which to direct your prayers. Nothing but a wall for wailing!"

Micah could hardly have imagined the LORD's temple replaced in its sacredness by nothing more than a retaining wall. Nor that prayers would be offered not *to* the wall but *through* the wall to a temple that no longer exists. Nor, less still, that today's wall of prayer would be half holy place, half tourist site.

It's not just the Jews, of course. I too know what it's like to "pray through a wall" to God, a wall which I myself have built because of my own disobedience or neglect. It is a wall that I usually have my back up against before I am forced in shame to come before God on my knees—a wall that separates me from God rather than brings me closer.

From hard experience, I know all too well what Amos meant when he cautioned that "in that day . . . the songs in the temple will turn to wailing." For those of us who have settled for unworthy substitutes, wailing comes in many forms.

As for the Jews, God finally could no longer bear their rebellion, and "in the end he thrust them from his presence." Inevitably, it meant the destruction of the temple, for it was not just the Babylonians or the Romans who sacked and burned the house of God. When the Jews rejected God (and later his chosen Messiah), it was as if the temple's very cornerstone had been ripped from its place, causing the building to collapse under the weight of the people's sin.

What then about you and me when we pull down God's temple through our own rebellion? Can we expect to once again come into his presence? Can we ever hope to rebuild a lasting relationship with God? Will not our friends rightly taunt us, like Sanballat sneering at the exiles who had returned to Jerusalem to rebuild the temple: "Can they bring the stones back to life from those heaps of rubble?"

The longer I stood at the Wailing Wall, the more I wanted to weep—first for my own sins, then for the sins of Israel. The bad news is that sin has forced us all from the presence of God. The good news is that we don't have to lift the heavy stones back into place. God has already done that, doing what we could never do: He has brought the stones back to life!

Jesus' critics couldn't understand it. Nor, sadly, those today who wail at the Western Wall. "Destroy this temple," Jesus said, "and I will raise it again in three days." Of course, the Jews of Jesus' day thought he was talking about Herod's temple. "It has taken forty-six years to build this temple, and you are going to raise it in three days?" they chided. But the temple of which Jesus had spoken was his own crucified body. One day it was as dead as the stone covering his tomb. Three days later it was brought back to life again by the incomparable power of his resurrection!

And here lies our own hope. Jesus' death and resurrection has made possible not only a new and more glorious temple, but a new and lasting presence in our lives. No more stones! No more walls! No more need for a compass-setting to find God! *Don't you know that you yourselves are God's temple and that God's Spirit lives in you?*

For just one fleeting moment I thought I could see, standing atop the Wailing Wall, the figure of King David, once again joyously proclaiming, "You turned my wailing into dancing!"

And as I walked further and further away from the wall into the old city of Jerusalem, I knew it was true: In leaving the wall, I had not taken even the first step away from God's presence.

Chapter Five

"It is more blessed

to give

than to receive."

Acts 20:35

Self-Centeredness

There I was, floating like a cork. No life preserver. No inner tube. No water wings. No effort. All the tour books said it would be like that, but whoever would have believed it? Naturally, there were trade-offs. The water was oily, and I didn't dare get any of it in my eyes, or swallow it. So normal swimming was out of the question. But I had not come to the Dead Sea to swim—only to float.

What I did manage to drink in safely while bobbing leisurely in this odd lake-masquerading-as-a-sea was the vast wasteland surrounding it. Wherever I looked, there was nothing but parched earth. Facing south, I could look to my right and almost see in the distance the craggy, 1400-foot ascent to the old Roman fortress of Masada.

Easily flipping myself around to face north, I could see to my left the historic site of the Qumran community, and above that the caves where the famous Dead Sea Scrolls were discovered. Ahead on my right and about 12 miles to the northeast was Mount Nebo, rising some 4000 feet above me. It was on Mount Nebo that Moses, after being told he couldn't enter the Promised Land, was given that tantalizingly quick peek of it.

From the spot where I was floating, I couldn't see the exact point at which the Jordan River emptied itself into the Dead Sea. Even so, I envisioned it like a stream of water running down into a stopped-up sink from a cold-water tap at the base of the Sea of Galilee, some 70 miles north.

Because the Dead Sea is more than 1300 feet below sea level (making it the lowest spot on the earth), there is no outlet for the incoming water. And because of the shimmering heat in the Negev Desert, the average four inches of rainfall each year evaporates almost before it hits the surface. The result is a body of water which is almost as solid as it is liquid. (At least 30 percent is mineral content, accounting for its other popular name, the Salt Sea.)

Not surprisingly, absolutely nothing can survive in these waters, whether fish, plants, or animals. The sea is literally as dead as its name implies.

What amazed me about the arid landscape on every side was knowing that the entire valley had at one time been extraordinarily green and fertile. In fact, it was so fertile that Abraham's nephew Lot had chosen this valley, reminiscent of the Garden of Eden in its lushness, as the prime location for his flocks and herds. "Lot looked up and saw that the whole plain of the Jordan was well watered, like the garden of the LORD."

Lush? Well-watered? Green? Fertile? Surely some salt had gotten into my eyes to blur reality. All I could see in any direction was scorched, dry, brown, and barren.

Only when you're right there in the middle of that dusty desert, and floating in "dead" water, as it were, can you begin to comprehend what a cataclysmic event it must have taken to bring about such a radical transition in the terrain. Only then can you fully appreciate the parenthetical note which Moses appended to Lot's view of the valley's lushness: "This was before the LORD destroyed Sodom and Gomorrah."

Sodom and Gomorrah. Fire and brimstone. Salt and sulfur. Now it all makes sense. For those who doubt whether God really did destroy those ancient cities with a rain of fire and brimstone, nothing could be stronger evidence than this unusual body of water and the surrounding desert.

In fact, because the southern part of the sea is extremely shallow, many have speculated that perhaps that area is the very plain where Sodom and Gomorrah were located. Seeds collected among burnt rocks on the southern perimeter of the sea indicate that it was once a fertile area producing wheat, barley, dates, grapes, figs, almonds, and olives—all supportive of the biblical account.

Do you, like me, find it both reassuring and disturbing to think that ancient biblical stories are true in every detail? Certainly I feel reassured to know that my faith rests not simply upon fictional myths but upon accurate, genuine historical narratives. Yet how can I not be disturbed by its implications for the seriousness of my sin and the inescapable reality of God's judgment?

I have to confess that sometimes I'm tempted to put God into two boxes. In one box is a harsh, judgmental God of the Old Testament, who—if I'm frank about it—I would never really want to meet face-to-face. In the other box is a gentle, gracious God of the New Testament who surely would have forgiven Sodom and Gomorrah rather than destroying them.

But I know that neither characterization is a true picture of God. After all, the "harsh God" of the Old Testament was willing to spare the two cities if even ten righteous souls could be found among the wicked; and he did in fact graciously save Lot and his family. As for the "forgiving God" of the New Testament, no one spoke more about hell (and its own association with fire and brimstone) than did Jesus himself—hardly the kind of soppy sentimentalist that we sometimes want him to be.

So I admit that my two little boxes are mostly self-serving. Too often I want to create God in my own image rather than be content simply to have been made in his. I want to be in control, especially when it comes to *me* and how I live my life.

The irony, of course, is that just such an attitude undergirded the wickedness of Sodom and Gomorrah. Yes, there was the notorious sexual perversion of the men of Sodom, but even this may have been more symptom than cause. Referring to the destruction of Sodom, Jesus once said that in the days of Lot "people were eating and drinking, buying and selling, planting and building." His obvious point—that the people of Sodom were unconcerned about judgment when it suddenly came upon them—should not overshadow the more compelling implication: Their very *busy-ness* implied an excessive *self-centeredness*.

We see this even more clearly in a passage in Deuteronomy which speaks of the punishment that awaited the nation of Israel should it violate its covenant with God: "The whole land will be a burning waste of salt and sulfur—nothing planted, nothing sprouting, no vegetation growing on it. It will be like the destruction of Sodom and Gomorrah. . . ."

What kind of attitude could possibly merit such Sodomlike punishment? An arrogance which says, "I will be safe, even though I persist in going my own way."

There it is again: Self-will; self-direction; self-centeredness. And the clincher comes when God speaks through Ezekiel, warning his people by saying, "Now this was the sin of your sister Sodom: She and her daughters were arrogant, overfed and unconcerned; they did not help the poor and needy." All they could think about was themselves. There was no giving, only taking.

Me. Me. Me. Nothing but me.

But wasn't the wickedness of Sodom the sin of sexual perversion? God's summary of Sodom's sin speaks volumes: "They were *haughty* and *did detestable things* before me." The connection could hardly be clearer. The "detestable things" they did (acts of sexual perversion) were the result of their "haughtiness" (their self-will and self-centeredness), which inevitably corrupted every part of their lives—social, ethical, and moral.

When one is bobbing up and down in a sea of salt, there is either little to think about or much to think about. The thought I could not dismiss that day was that sin—all sin, whether disgusting and gross or all-too-acceptable—finds its source in an excessive attention to self.

Attributing the existence of the Dead Sea to the single sin of sexual perversion is certainly convenient. It lets most of us off the hook. But attributing its existence to the sin of *self-centeredness* indicts us all.

No, more than that, it *explains* all. It tells me more than I want to know about why I am not as happy as I would like to be; about why I'm not as fulfilled as I know I could be; about why I sometimes feel more dead than alive.

I don't know how I keep missing it. It's been right there in the words of the hymn "There Is a Sea," which I've sung all my life.

It's the story of the life-giving Sea of Galilee and the almost useless
Dead Sea:

> There is a sea which day by day receives the rippling rills,
> And streams that spring from wells of God, or fall from
>   cedared hills;
> But what it thus receives it gives, with glad
>   unsparing hand:
> A stream more wide, with deeper tide, flows on to lower land.
>
> There is a sea which day by day receives a fuller tide;
> But all its store it keeps, nor gives to shore nor sea beside;
> Its Jordan stream, now turned to brine, lies heavy as
>   molten lead;
> Its dreadful name doth e'er proclaim, that sea is waste
>   and dead.

The first two stanzas of the hymn were given to us by an unknown
writer. The third stanza, written by Lula Klingman Zahn, tells us beauti-
fully which sea God is like and lays down a challenge for each of us:

> Which shall it be for you and me, who God's good gifts obtain?
> Shall we accept for self alone, or take to give again?
> For He who once was rich indeed laid all His glory down;
> That by His grace our ransomed race
> Should share His wealth and crown.

Are you unhappy? Do you long for greater purpose and fulfill-
ment? Do you often feel more dead than alive? If so, it's time to do

some serious bobbing in the Dead Sea and to think long and hard about just how much our lives are wrapped up in ourselves: in our careers, in our clothes, in our houses, in our money, in all the things that keep us looking inward instead of outward.

That was the very problem of Lot's wife. When she looked back as she fled from Sodom, there was something about her life that she just couldn't let go of. Was she simply too tied to her house, or to her material luxuries, or to her social aspirations to give them all up? Whatever it was, it turned her into a pillar of salt. No wonder Jesus told us to "remember Lot's wife!"

According to Jesus, the fate of Lot's wife is once again the lesson of the two seas: *"Whoever tries to keep his life will lose it, and whoever loses his life will preserve it."*

Which sea are you most like? Which sea would you like to be? Maybe it's time for a sea-change in your life. I suppose one could get used to just floating, but wouldn't you really rather *swim*?

Chapter Six

"Dry bones,

hear the word

of the LORD."

EZEKIEL 37:4

Extravagance

Death seems to cradle the Kidron Valley in its lap. On both sides of the deep ravine which runs between Jerusalem's east wall and the Mount of Olives are two graveyards. Looming over the eastern side of the Valley is by far the larger of the two, a vast Jewish burial site with wall-to-wall white tombs dating back to ancient times. Two of the more prominent cemetery structures have tall, columned facades, concealing burial caves and bone boxes, called ossuaries.

Tantalizingly out of reach in one of the tombs is what has been described as an otherwise-ordinary-looking box of bones marked simply "Mary and Martha." In Israel, such common names should not cause any particular excitement—except for the fact that this particular ancient burial site is not just on the brow of the Kidron Valley, but is also just this side of the hill from Bethany. . . .

Bethany? Mary and Martha? The mind races. Could it be? Is it possible? Might these bones actually be the skeletal remains of Lazarus' sisters, Mary and Martha?

My first thought was, "Thank you, Lord, that no one has desecrated this spot with some touristy shrine!" My second thought was, "Thank you, Lord, that you yourself have enshrined the memory of these two women of God—yes, perhaps in these very bones but without question in the deep recesses of my own memory. Indeed, in the world's memory!

Did not Matthew tell us in his Gospel that Jesus had said of Mary, "I tell you the truth, wherever the gospel is preached throughout the world, what she has done will also be told, in memory of her"?

How, then, could anyone forget Mary? For that matter, how could anyone forget Martha? After all, they were sisters, spoken of almost in the same breath. Yet the irony of their story, and perhaps of these very bones lying next to each other in the same burial box, is that they were two quite different women. Like so many siblings who come from the same womb and who share many of the same family traits, Mary and Martha are remembered as much for their differences as for their similarities.

From what we know, both Mary and Martha were godly women. Martha, particularly, was known for her hospitality and her penchant for serving. Perhaps unfairly, I also see her as a fastidious hostess, paying attention to every detail, from the perfect preparation of the food to making sure that the length of the tablecloth was precisely correct on all sides. For Martha, everything had to be right. Just the right menu. Just the right flowers. Just the right touch.

Jesus must have felt comfortably ensconced when Martha opened her home to him on his way from Galilee into Judea. Martha was treating him royally, in a manner fit for the king that he was. But you know the rest of the story as well as I. While Martha is busy about the kitchen, Mary excuses herself (or maybe is too eager even to bother) and joins the other guests. Oblivious to the clatter in the kitchen, Mary sits at Jesus' feet, absorbed in his very presence, taking in every word, drinking in the wine of his wisdom, mesmerized with his spiritual insight, when suddenly Martha bursts from the kitchen and startles everyone: "Lord, don't you care that my sister has left me to do the work by myself? Tell her to help me!"

You can almost hear the resounding silence that followed. What is Jesus to do? He is, after all, Martha's guest, and it is, after all, Martha who has been slaving away in preparation of what is sure to be a wonderful meal. But just when we might assume Jesus would turn to Mary and say, "Perhaps we can talk later. It looks like Martha could use some help for the moment," Jesus turns to Martha instead, and rebukes her! "Martha, Martha," he said, "you are worried and upset about many things, but only one thing is needed. Mary has chosen what is better, and it will not be taken away from her."

Jesus might just as well have said bluntly, "Martha, you're nothing but a worrywart! Can't you get out of your ordinary routine long enough to see the far greater power that God is wanting to bring into your life?"

Wouldn't you love to have been a fly on the wall and seen the expression on Martha's face? Indeed, wouldn't you love to have seen the expression on *Mary's* face as well! Surely Mary politely retreated into the kitchen in spite of Jesus' bold defense. Didn't she? And surely Martha swallowed her embarrassment and quickly disarmed any tension on the part of her guests by taking her place at Jesus' feet, where Mary had been.

What else are we to imagine, knowing as we do that Jesus' rebuke did not destroy their warm friendship? When dinner was finally served, you just know it was a wonderful, relaxed feast of food and fellowship—with, of course, the tablecloth draped precisely at just the right length all around!

There is much that could be made of that intriguing incident, but we must not rush to judgment. There are two other occasions involving these fascinating sisters that reveal even more about how they were so different.

There is, first of all, the death of their brother Lazarus and the belated arrival of Jesus four days after Lazarus' passing. Have you ever noticed that wonderfully delicious detail which John gives us about Martha's reaction when Jesus orders the gravestone to be taken away? Remember that, just minutes before, Martha had acknowledged Jesus as "the Christ, the Son of God, who was to come into the world." She also had just told Jesus, "Lord, if you had been here, my brother would not have died. But I know that even now God will give you whatever you ask."

Yet as the gravestone is about to be rolled from its place, Martha reverts almost instinctively to her persnickety self. "But, Lord," Martha fairly whispers (undoubtedly glancing over her shoulder to see if anyone might be overhearing her), "Lord, by this time there is a bad odor, for he has been there four days."

On the brink of what surely must be the second-most-stirring resurrection ever to be recorded, Martha is worried about the *odor*! Can you imagine it? Jesus is about to bring her brother from death back to life, and all Martha can think about is the stench of decay within the tomb! "Martha, Martha," Jesus must have thought once again, "you are worried and upset about many things, but only one thing is needed." Jesus surely had great patience. This time there was no rebuke, but only the simple reminder, "Did I not tell you that if you believed, you would see the glory of God?"

In fairness to Martha, how would you and I react today if we were told that a loved one was about to be brought to life after being buried for four days? Maybe we wouldn't worry about the odor—just about the uncertain specter of viewing again the body which we had held so dear before death robbed us cruelly of its warmth and vitality. Yet quite apart from awkward grave scenes, do we, like Martha, worry more about appearances than trusting in God?

There is then that final story, when Jesus returns to Bethany in the last week before his own death. Jesus is once again the guest of honor at a banquet, this time in the home of Simon the Leper. And look who is serving the meal, even in Simon's house: It's Martha! And what is Mary doing while Martha is in the kitchen? Anointing Jesus with an expensive perfume and getting criticized by Judas and some of the other disciples for her incredible wastefulness!

Even within the short time since the miraculous resurrection of Lazarus, it's back to form for both sisters. For her part, Martha is once again busy serving. Indeed, who could fault her? Serving is a Christian calling. But Mary understands something that Martha keeps missing—the special blessing of the Lord's very real presence in her life. And thus Mary serves in a radically different way than does her sister—not with neatness and propriety, but with an overwhelming profusion of love!

Two sisters, alike in so many ways, could hardly be more different in their service to God. For Martha, it meant always doing what was right and proper and expected—whatever might be thought of as "the Christian thing to do." For Mary, godly service meant not just dutiful hospitality or expected works of charity or even generous acts of kindness, but an outpouring of love and adoration that was . . . well, truly extravagant!

Where Martha was worried about appearances, and propriety, and social expectations, Mary completely lost herself in spiritual passion! Where Martha was concerned about *things*, Mary was concerned about *people*, and especially the personhood of God. Where Martha was worried about neatness and correctness and the odor of death, Mary exulted lavishly—yes, even sacrificially—in the fragrance of life!

As I think about the lessons to be learned from a box of ancient bones near Bethany, I can't help but think that there is more to be learned than the fascinating difference between two sisters who lived centuries ago. Or even the difference between dutiful service and passionate adoration, or the radical difference between even generous acts of charity and unbounded spiritual extravagance. (From what Mary and Martha have taught me, how could I ever again think that good works alone are worthy of my Savior? How could I possibly ever come into the presence of God with anything but unbridled spiritual passion?)

Yet isn't the real story of Mary and Martha a story about how God views you and me? Unlike Martha, God doesn't get hung up on the details. He doesn't care whether I'm rich or poor, black or white, high society or working class. Oh, you can count on heaven being the grandest banquet ever prepared, with every tablecloth hanging perfectly right and not a single detail overlooked. Our God is indeed a God of details! But other than in matters of purity and obedience, God couldn't care less about our own appearances. He looks not upon the outward man but the inward. He doesn't care who we are on the outside, but who we are on the inside.

And what could be more wonderful than the thought that, like the passionate Mary, God too has poured out his love for us so extravagantly on the cross—giving the lifeblood of his own Son to anoint us head to toe with his priceless mercy!

With love like that—love so extraordinary, so extravagant—how dare we get so wrapped up in the busy activities of even godly Christian service that we fail to recognize the passionate presence of God in our lives this very day?

> *Were the whole realm of nature mine,*
> *That were a present far too small;*
> *Love so amazing, so divine,*
> *Demands my soul, my life, my all.*
>
> —*Isaac Watts*
> *(1674-1748)*

Chapter Seven

"We are being

renewed

day by day."

2 CORINTHIANS 4:16

Renewal

It was yet another surprise in this land of constant surprises. Certainly I never would have expected to find anything like it near the Dead Sea. But the sign along the road leading south to Masada indicated that a right turn would take us to the En Gedi Reserve. "A *game reserve? Here?*" I remember thinking.

An information board beside the entry booth promised a wide variety of flora and fauna. Apparently the En Gedi has always been known for its unique beauty. Only when I read the park brochure was I reminded that, in his Song of Songs, Solomon had likened his beloved to "a cluster of henna blossoms from the vineyards of En Gedi." Sadly, the fragrance of henna (said to be like roses) never presented itself.

Among the animals listed as being featured in the reserve were the long-horned ibex (a deerlike species of mountain goat) and the huggable little rock hyrax (the biblical rabbit).

The trail ahead was supposed to lead to several waterfalls along what was known as David's Wadi (or stream). As advertised, the path winding up the rapidly rising cliffs followed alongside a narrow stream with crystal-clear water in it, and there were various pools and waterfalls along the way.

The higher we climbed, the closer we got to a particularly beautiful waterfall, which cascaded down some 700 feet from a point where the stream was fed by four springs. When we finally reached the foot of the falls and looked up, we could see an unusual draping of mossy grass along the top of the falls, like long tresses hanging down a woman's back.

Apparently someone else had had the same idea, for the sign at the base of the falls reads "Shulamit Falls," perhaps a reference to Abishag, the beautiful young Shulamit (or Shunammite) girl who was summoned to lie next to King David when he was old and unable to keep warm. (Some believe she is the same "Shulammite" of whom Solomon wrote in his Song of Songs. Others link the fall's name to a star, which name itself probably takes us back to the biblical text.)

Naming this beautiful waterfall after the beautiful Abishag would certainly have been appropriate. Just as she was a comfort to David in his old age, these very falls may well have been a source of great solace to David in his younger years.

We know that, while hiding out from an angry King Saul, David "lived in the strongholds of En Gedi." We also know that Saul was told, "'David is in the Desert of En Gedi.' So Saul took three thousand chosen men from all Israel and set out to look for David and his men near the Crags of the Wild Goats."

That pretty much pinpoints the spot where I was standing as being right in the center of David's stronghold. In fact, I could look up on every side and see caves like those in which David and his men must have hidden. (It was in just such a cave, remember, that David cut off the corner of Saul's robe instead of killing him.) So it isn't much of a stretch to think that David might have found the Shulamit Falls to be a source of refreshment and comfort while he was being hotly pursued by Saul.

If there is any irony about the apparent naming of Shulamit Falls, it is that Abishag brought David warmth when he was old and cold, while the falls at En Gedi brought a much younger David cool refreshment in the desert heat. More than irony, it just might explain why we are given that ever-so-intriguing account of Abishag and David.

The story couldn't be briefer, nor in some ways stranger. When David was old and couldn't keep warm, his servants decided to look for a young virgin to lie beside him. "Then they searched throughout Israel for a beautiful girl and found Abishag, a Shunammite, and brought her to the king. The girl was very beautiful; she took care of the king and waited on him, but the king had no intimate relations with her."

Even given the days of polygamy and concubines, this surely must be a strange story. Were there no primitive bed warmers in that time? Indeed, why didn't Bathsheba sleep beside David to provide the needed warmth?

We may never learn the answers to those questions, but the more I read my Bible, the more convinced I am that there are no throwaway lines in Scripture. Every word there is meant to tell us more about God.

Could it be that God wants us to know through every means possible—whether by revelation or by nature itself—that he is our oasis of refuge and comfort in time of need? *Whatever our need?* If it is for warmth when we are cold, he gives us warmth. If it is for cool refreshment when we are hot, he gives us cool refreshment.

Perhaps he meets our physical needs just that literally at times. Far more importantly, of course, he meets our spiritual needs, whatever they may be.

The safety and tranquility of this place must have been as spiritually refreshing to David as it was physically refreshing. One can imagine that, soothed by the sounds of the waterfall, David might well have become lost in a quiet reverie, wistfully reflecting back on the days when he "used to go with the multitude, leading the procession to the house of God, with shouts of joy and thanksgiving among the festive throng," as expressed by the sons of Korah in Psalm 42.

But for now he was in exile. For now he was a man on the run, an outlaw in hiding. No admiring multitudes here. No grand processions. No shouts of joy.

As I sat down inside a natural archway formed by the tall grasses at the wadi's edge and felt surprising coolness surround me, I wondered whether David might have sat in that very spot and felt that same coolness. If so, what a refreshing refuge it would have been for him—not just from the heat of the desert, but even more so from the heat of his conflict with someone who had been his mentor and friend. Saul's betrayal must surely have been a bitter pill for David.

Have you ever felt betrayed? Perhaps by a close friend, or a spiritual leader, or maybe even by a spouse or some other family member? I have. More than once. And nothing hurts worse. I dare say that most of us can step into David's sandals and know at least something of the pain he must have felt—something of what it is like to be attacked or to be estranged by one's least likely enemy.

"Whatever happened to the hugs, the smiles, the good times together?" we ask. One day it's flowers and candy; the next day it's nothing but cold shoulders. For David, it was a high-ranking position in Saul's army on one day and Saul's spear being hurled at him the next. Who can make any sense of such sudden turnabouts?

I think that, for me, what hurts most may be the loss of trust. If we can't trust those nearest and dearest to us, then who *can* we trust?

Or is it the rejection that hurts most? What could be more devastating than being rejected by those who claim to love us—to be casually tossed aside as if we were never anything more than a play toy for someone else's enjoyment?

What else are we to think? As long as we are useful, we are considered a friend; but beyond the point of usefulness, we are expendable—as easily tossed aside as a discarded candy wrapper.

In the cool of the shade, I recalled the various times when I have felt betrayed and rejected. I couldn't help but appreciate the contrasting picture of God's constancy and faithfulness as so wonderfully represented by this refreshing oasis in the midst of a desert.

When we *need* an oasis, God *gives* us an oasis. When we *need* refuge and comfort, God *gives* us refuge and comfort.

I like to think that, sitting at the foot of Shulamit Falls, David had been given an oasis of refuge and comfort, and that his soul was refreshed. I knew right then and there that mine was.

Suddenly, out of the corner of my eye, I noticed several young ibex working their way slowly toward the stream nearby. One by one they began to lower their heads to take a drink from the cool water. As I watched them for a few minutes, I kept thinking that they were more like young deer than mountain goats. Could this pool and just such a scene as I was watching possibly have inspired the writer of the 42nd Psalm?

Hardly any words have become more familiar:

As the deer pants for streams of water,
so my soul pants for you, O God.

Rarely have words told of more agony:

My tears have been my
food day and night,
while men say to me all day long,
"Where is your God?"

Seldom has hope been so present in the midst of despair:

Why are you downcast, O my soul?
Why so disturbed within me?
Put your hope in God,
For I will yet praise him,
My Savior and my God.

I have been in this situation too: betrayed, downcast, fearful, disturbed. Can I not, then, share in this renewed hope? Am I not able to say, "I will yet praise him"? Can I not know that same peace when all around me is turmoil?

Deep calls to deep
in the roar of your waterfalls;

all your waves and breakers
have swept over me.

By day the LORD *directs his love,*
at night his song is with me—
a prayer to the God of my life.

No wonder, then, that we love to sing Martin Nystrom's adaptation of the 42nd Psalm:

As the deer pants for the water,
So my soul longs after You.
You alone are my heart's desire
And I long to worship you.

You alone are my strength, my shield,
To You alone may my spirit yield.
You alone are my heart's desire
And I long to worship you.

Does your soul thirst for a living God? I can tell you this: Having been to David's Wadi and been spiritually refreshed, I'll never again sing that song in quite the same way. Now, there will always be a roaring waterfall in the background, and a cool, re-freshing stream, and the ever-present assurance that God meets my needs. *All* my needs! Every one!

Chapter Eight

"He who

watches over you

will not slumber."

PSALM 121:3

Priorities

Shabbat in Jerusalem. The Sabbath. This morning a congregation of Messianic Jews (Jewish Christians) gathers for worship. At first blush it is like any other synagogue worship in the city today, complete with traditional yarmulkes and prayer shawls, and the Torah scroll being reverently passed around the room for all the worshipers to touch.

There will be another service tomorrow, on the first day of the week, for more prayer, more singing, and more teaching from the Scriptures, but especially for gathering around the Lord's table in memory of Yeshua Mashiach—Jesus, the crucified and risen Messiah of prophecy.

For anyone accustomed to traditional Christian worship, the worship of Jewish believers can come as a shock. It's like being hurled back 2000 years to the first century, complete with the chanting of the Hebrew Torah; the singing of the psalms accompanied not with instruments but often with vigorous clapping; the openness to discussion (even debate!) following the "sermon"; and the informal passing of the matza (unleavened bread) and wine during the Lord's supper.

But it is not just the style of worship that is different. There are also ritual differences, and observances, feasts, and religious practices completely foreign to Gentile Christians. I almost have to pinch myself to make sure I am not back in the first century attending the crucial "Jerusalem conference" in which significant differences between Jewish and Gentile believers were hammered out.

Many of the questions remain the same: Must Christians practice circumcision? Are we to eat only kosher food? Is the Sabbath to be observed?

If the answers to those questions seem to be an all-too-obvious "no" to Gentile believers, they are an unequivocal "yes" for most Jewish believers. To be a Jewish believer is to be both a *believer* and *Jewish*—Jewish right down to practicing circumcision, eating kosher, and observing the Sabbath! Does not one continue to be a Jew even after he or she becomes a believer? And don't all Jews observe the Sabbath?

Observance of the Sabbath is never more noticeable than when one is in Jerusalem on Shabbat. On Shabbat the city simply shuts down. The shops close, the buses don't run, and—except for the Arab sections of the city, or the odd Chinese or fast-food establishment—you can forget having a meal in a restaurant. In the Mea She'arim area this morning, even the streets were barricaded so that unwary tourists like myself wouldn't have our cars stoned by the ultra-Orthodox. It is Shabbat! "Thou shalt do no work on the Sabbath!"

You get some idea about the seriousness of Sabbath restrictions when you learn that, for more zealous Jews, even pushing a button on an elevator is forbidden. Yet you wonder a bit about the consistency of all the strict lawkeeping when you discover that the elevators have been programmed to stop on every floor, allowing passengers to do no more than walk off on whatever floor they choose!

The intricacies of the Sabbath rituals swirled through the theological side of my brain as I entered the Jaffa Gate for a Saturday afternoon walk through the Old City. The contrast between the Jewish Sabbath and the business-as-usual atmosphere of the Arab quarter could not have been more striking. Most of the Arab merchants keep their shops open seven days a week, even if they might close briefly on their own Friday Sabbath for the call to prayer.

In the souks (those rambling narrow market streets of the Old City filled with every kind of wares imaginable), tourists like myself were not only tolerated but welcomed. With the passing of each stall came the now-familiar touting of the merchants. After the umpteenth sales pitch, the enforced inactivity and quiet of the Jewish Sabbath started looking awfully good!

To escape the raucous commercialism, I headed for the peacefulness of St. Anne Church on the east side of the Old City, and more particularly for the Pool of Bethesda (or Bethsaida) immediately adjacent to it. These days there is little left of the pool but ancient ruins. Certainly no water, and no throngs of sick people hoping to take advantage of what was once considered the pool's medicinal healing power.

Still, it's easy to see what a magnificent place the Pool of Bethesda once was. Some of the decorative columns are still standing, and numerous flights of stone steps still lead down to what would have been the bottom of the pool. On this day the ancient stones were graced with an overgrowth of brilliant red poppies, rather more suitable for a picture postcard than for a bathing pool. However, in its own way the view itself was soothing, almost healing.

Climbing a number of steps to the upper side of the pool, I sat down and quietly took in the view.

Having mentally reconstructed the ancient pool, I reached for my Bible and turned to John's account of the most famous incident ever associated with this center of health and healing. In the fifth chapter of his Gospel, John tells of a conversation between Jesus and a man who had been an invalid for 38 years. Seeing the man lying by the pool, Jesus asked if he wanted to get well. "Sir," the invalid replied, "I have no one to help me into the pool when the water is stirred. While I am trying to get in, someone else goes down ahead of me."

At that point Jesus spoke the words that came back to me even from early Sunday school flannel-board lessons: "Get up! Pick up your mat and walk." Then John tells us, "At once the man was cured; he picked up his mat and walked." For me as a young boy growing up, the image of a crippled man jumping up and walking was exciting indeed. But somehow I had missed the excitement of the controversy which ensued.

That controversy is introduced in the very next verse, which says simply: "The day on which this took place was a Sabbath." From what I had already experienced in Jerusalem that day, I now realized that both Jesus and the man whom he had healed were in deep trouble. Even to my Gentile mind, it sounded like far too much work going on to satisfy the self-appointed enforcers of Shabbat. Sure enough, as John tells us, the Jews said to the man who had been healed, "It is the Sabbath; the law forbids you to carry your mat."

Of course, it wasn't just mat-carrying that they were so exercised about. In a later incident, the "Sabbath police" faulted Jesus for the very act of *healing* on the Sabbath! Luke's Gospel tells us that "the Pharisees and the teachers of the law were looking for a reason to accuse Jesus, so they watched him closely to see if he would heal on the Sabbath." In Matthew they even asked Jesus point-blank, "Is it lawful to heal on the Sabbath?"

Can you believe it? There were people in Jesus' day who thought that the meticulous observance of the law was more important than healing an invalid! Such an attitude fairly boggles the mind, doesn't it? Or does it?

If we're honest about it, there are too many times when we ourselves have virtually the same attitude. No, not about the *Sabbath*, but about *people*. Remember when Jesus was rebuked for permitting his hungry disciples to pick and eat grain on the Sabbath? Jesus' response was as breathtaking as it was brief: "The Sabbath was made for man, not man for the Sabbath."

We shouldn't think that Jesus was somehow nullifying the Sabbath principle. What he was telling the Jews, and us, is that God's laws are always given to us for our own good. Without a regular day of rest and worshipful reflection, we suffer in both body and soul. But if such a day is meant for our own good, then what could possibly be a greater good than for the lame to walk, the blind to see, or the hungry to be fed?

Simply put, the Sabbath principle is: people first! If that normally means observing a day of rest for the good of most people, for others it may sometimes mean an act of work.

It's a matter of priorities. Religious ritual is good, but showing mercy is even better. And, where not otherwise in violation of God's specific commands, it is *people* who ought to receive the highest priority—not laws, not traditions, not our busy schedules, not our money, not our careers, nor any of a multitude of other things that seem so important to us. It is precisely here—in wrongly prioritizing *things* over *people*—that we so often run afoul of the Sabbath principle.

For me, it may be the student who drops by the office in need of encouragement when the deadline for getting a manuscript in the mail is just minutes away. For someone else, it may be the unexpected visitors who knock at the door when the house is too messy to invite them in. Or perhaps it's a child who asks yet another question in a never-ending string of questions when something is on television that just can't be missed.

As I sat at the top of the steps leading down into the Pool of Bethesda, I was struck with my own part in the story of the lame man. I'm the one who shoved him out of the way in my own rush to get into the pool! In so many ways every day, I run ahead of those with greater needs, leaving them emotionally crippled, intellectually blind, and spiritually hungry. Worse yet, like the most zealous of "Sabbath police," I too can rationalize my behavior with the noblest of motives. Even with Scripture, if necessary!

Just then I saw something in the text which I had never seen before. It was something Jesus said when he was rebuked for healing on the Sabbath. "My Father," said Jesus, "is always at his work."

God, *always at his work?*

What an incredible thought! The Creator of the universe, who rested from all his labors on the seventh day, has never rested since! "The Sabbath was made for man" because we need our rest; but it was not made for God, because God needs no rest. And, unlike us, God never gets his priorities mixed up. With God, our needs always come first.

So there I was on a Sabbath at the Pool of Bethesda, sinful and lame and in need of healing. And suddenly the waters of my soul were stirred with a wonderful thought—that, when it comes to doing whatever is best for us, our Father never takes a day off!

How then could I ever miss the point? When it comes to my own life, I should endeavor to become an increasingly better rule-keeper. In ways we too often fail to appreciate, God's rules are meant for our own good. But within the hierarchy of God's values, mercy always trumps the letter of the law. As Jesus himself demonstrated, when it comes to serving the needs of others, some rules are indeed made to be broken!

Chapter Nine

"Restore us,

O God."

PSALM 80:3

Restoration

I assumed it would be like all the other model villages I had seen. Among my favorite childhood memories was a model that stood in the middle of a public park in Winnipeg, Manitoba. Later, in my travels to England, I was enthralled by a large model village in the Devon beach town of Babbacombe, near Torquay, and an even more intricate one in Bourton-on-the-Water, the well-known tourist spot close to our cottage in the Cotswolds. That one has a tiny model village *within* the model village, exactly where it is in the actual village!

So what else would this outdoor model be but yet another fascinating little toy town, with houses, streets, and other structures duplicated in miniature scale, to the delight of both children and adults?

What I discovered in Jerusalem at the Model of the Second Temple was anything but what I had expected. It was like walking back in time, to the days of Christ.

For almost a week I had been wandering around the Old City in search of various significant sites, only to get hopelessly lost, particularly in the Arab quarter with its complex maze of souks crowded with merchants and shoppers. Even when I was guided by my friend Joseph, I could hardly make sense of all the ruins he would show me: a wall from the time of Ezra here; a column from the Byzantine era there; a Crusader building over here; a street built by Herod over there. Ruins and rubble. Ruins and rubble. By the end of a week in the Old City, Jerusalem was beginning to look like little more than ruins and rubble.

How is a person ever to get a feel for the reality of the first-century world of Jesus and the apostles when it lies mostly buried under layer upon layer of political and military conflict? Where does a person begin to get his bearings when one ancient wall has been replaced by another, more modern, one; and that one replaced by yet another?

Even more frustrating are the many sites of biblical interest which are today covered over by some ecclesiastical structure. How is anyone to appreciate what the original scene must have looked like when it is camouflaged by stained glass and marble? And what could be more ironic? In an attempt to preserve the holy places of history, the church itself has often been most responsible for obscuring the view!

You can imagine, then, how thrilling it was to find this model of ancient Jerusalem, constructed under the direction of a team of archaeological, literary, and biblical scholars. As far as possible, it is even constructed of the original materials used at the time, including marble, stone, wood, copper, and iron. (Heim Perez, the man who actually built the model, proudly handed me a small piece of the marble to carry home.)

At last it all made sense. At a scale of 1 to 50, you could almost believe that you were hovering above the Old City in a helicopter. Look! There is Herod's Palace and Pilate's residence in the same luxurious complex. And over there is Caiaphas' house, where Jesus was first brought after being arrested. With but the slightest imagination, you can almost see Jesus as he is being led back and forth through the city during the long night of his arrest and trial.

For me, the highlight of the model was the second temple itself—the one originally built by Ezra and renovated by Herod. Despite reading about its construction and generally knowing its layout and dimensions, my mind still couldn't quite grasp what the temple must have looked like in the first century or how it related to the City of David or to Mount Zion.

Perhaps nothing more obscures one's attempt to picture the second temple in its original state than a prior visit to Temple Mount, dominated as it is today by the El Aqsa Mosque and the attention-grabbing Dome of the Rock. Without the Model of the second temple to bring one back to first-century reality, one might never fully appreciate how imposing the second temple used to be on that very site.

But it was not just the temple's dominance of the model city that was surprising; it was also the detail. Peering right down into the temple grounds, you can see a wall separating the court of the Gentiles from the area where only Jews were permitted to enter. So *that's* the "wall of separation" between Jews and Gentiles that was torn down by Jesus' death on the cross! (Or at least the wall from which the figure of speech was drawn.)

And look! On the north side of the temple is the Fortress of Antonio and the door leading from the Roman barracks out onto the top of the temple portico. It was probably through that very door that Paul was taken so that he could make his defense to the rioting crowd that had caused him to be arrested. Without the model, I would never have known how close the barracks were to the temple.

With each street, structure, and view, the biblical Jerusalem I have read about over and over again for a lifetime began to come alive. Only when I looked over and saw a cat taking a drink from the Pool of Bethesda was I brought back to reality! It was, indeed, only a model. But how very close it must be to the real thing!

With a model we can see "the real thing," the genuine article. No additives. No tawdry substitutes. That's the kind of Christianity I want—just biblical Christianity at its very best!

The good news is that we *do* have a model. It's the New Testament church itself, built on the foundation of Jesus and the Spirit-led apostles. What more do we need? Why all the accumulated centuries of dogma, creeds, encyclicals, synods, conventions, and church traditions? It's like taking first-century Jerusalem and adding more walls. Expensive walls. Burdensome walls. Divisive walls. Walls that obscure Christ himself and make it almost impossible for me to rediscover the true heart and soul of Christian faith.

The authenticity and simplicity of the model struck a deep chord in me. For in my own life I see areas in need of spiritual restoration. With few exceptions, what I see is mostly ruin and rubble, ruin and rubble.

Oh, I've built with good intentions. And there are times when I can look back and see my life "in its glory," if you will. It was a time of innocence, of purity, of youthful commitment and spiritual idealism. But time and the world have a way of eroding whatever we build.

In fact, the natural world seems to prefer ruin and rubble to temples and towers. Through every force at its command, nature takes sinister pleasure in cracking, crumbling, eroding, and rusting our best efforts to build that which will endure through time.

Sadly, my spiritual life has been no exception. Just when I thought my life in Christ was secure, I began to notice telltale cracks, then serious crumbling. At times I hardly recognize myself, and it's not just the natural erosion caused by living in an evil world. No, I've actually been so bold as to intentionally re-design and rebuild, thinking that maybe I could improve on the pattern.

Sometimes I've even thought that the model which I had always followed was outdated, somehow embarrassingly out of step with the times. But at these times I realize I'm building on shifting sand, and not on the Rock. How then could I ever expect anything else but ruin and rubble?

So for me it's back to basics, where I can make sense of my life. Back to biblical Christianity, where no religious traditions can obscure my view of what God has called me to be. Back to the un-abashed idealism of my youth and to the commitment of faith which I sometimes ignore.

By the grace of God I will one day return to the Old City of Jerusalem, and walk again amidst the ruin and rubble that time and armies have not yet managed to destroy. It's a city that captures your soul.

But when I'm old and unable to walk, take me back to the miniature model, where my dimming eyes can catch a last squinting glimpse of the Jerusalem of Jesus. No ruins. No rubble. No embell-ishment. No golden domes of a religion which denies the very deity of Christ!

Give me one last taste of "the real thing."

And then let me rest restored in the shadow of Jesus, the great Builder and Architect of an eternal Jerusalem—where there will be no more ruins or rubble, and where I shall walk forever on streets of purest gold.

Chapter Ten

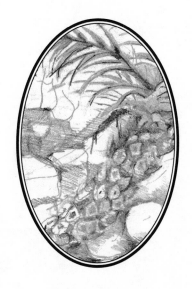

"Create in me

a pure heart,

O God."

PSALM 51:10

Purity

Mention the name *Qumran* and you are likely to get blank stares. Mention the *Dead Sea Scrolls* and you might just see a glimmer of recognition. Depending on who you're talking to, you might even get a look of excited envy, as in, "Wow, you've seen the Dead Sea Scrolls?"

For the uninitiated, the Dead Sea Scrolls are one of the greatest archaeological discoveries of the century. Among other writings, they contain the world's oldest manuscripts of the Hebrew Bible—the Old Testament—which have confirmed the authenticity of far more recent copies of the original text. For biblical scholars, it's exciting stuff indeed!

Yet it is somewhat misleading to speak in terms of an "archaeological" find. Discovery of the first scrolls was made in 1947 by a young Bedouin shepherd boy looking for a stray goat. Fortuitously, in a cave high above the desert floor beside the Dead Sea (from which the scrolls take their name), he found clay jars containing the historic scrolls. Only after some cloak-and-dagger intrigue worthy of Hollywood were the other manuscripts eventually discovered by archaeologists.

In addition to the ancient manuscripts of the Bible, there were also other writings which help explain what the scrolls were doing in the caves in the first place. These texts (from as early as the first century B.C.) tell us much about the Essenes, a breakaway Jewish community of pious superpatriots who had abandoned Jerusalem in 200 B.C. to live a monastic lifestyle in the desert.

From what can be pieced together, the Essenes apparently were the educated elite from the temple hierarchy, who were upset when the Jewish Hashmonite dynasty refused to appoint one of their number as the high priest. Thus alienated from the Hashmonites, as well as the occupying Romans, the Essenes retreated to what was supposed to be a temporary "Mount Zion," to await the redemption of Israel and the coming of the Messiah of prophecy.

For some two centuries the Essenes maintained an Armageddonlike vision of the "end of time" when they, the "Sons of Light," would defeat the "Sons of Darkness." However, that victory was never to be. In A.D. 68, just before the fall of Jerusalem, the Essenes were all but wiped out by the Roman legions.

It was in a small settlement at the base of the caves where the scrolls were found that the Essenes had set up their community in exile, known today as Qumran. Every hour of their day was regimented: eight hours of sleep; eight of work; eight of study. In the ruins which one can see partially restored today, two prominent features highlight the community's dual dedication to personal purity and to the preservation of the written Word of God.

The first feature of the ruins is a room known as the scriptorium, where the manuscripts were painstakingly copied. I was amazed to see in that room a smoothly plastered desk, as well as ceramic and bronze inkwells. Using only a little imagination, I could almost see the ancient scribes busily at work, straining to make sure that every "i" was dotted and every "t" was crossed.

Apparently that same discipline was characteristic of their personal lives. Known as the "Pious Ones," the Essenes also strained to dot every "i" and cross every "t" when it came to observing ritual purity. For the Essenes, cleanliness was indeed next to godliness!

Nothing evidences that commitment more than the second central feature of the ruins—a large cistern supplying collected rainwater to a number of *mikvehs*, or ritual baths. Without the *mikvehs*, the Essenes' many ceremonial washings simply would not have been possible. One has to visit the ruins in person to fully appreciate the ingenuity that went into building such an incredible water system in the midst of the desert.

Following a strict set of purity rules, the Essenes immersed themselves in the *mikveh* at least five times a day, including each time they would go to the toilet. Also, a ritual bath was required both before and after a scribe could copy the sacred name of Jehovah God (perhaps partially explaining why ancient biblical scrolls were so rare and expensive).

Yet one should not think that the *mikveh* experience was limited to the Essenes. I was impressed, for example, with the Jewish *mikvehs* at Masada, to the south of Qumran. One *mikveh* in particular presented a sharp contrast to the licentious paganism of the Romans. Dug immediately adjacent to the elaborate Roman bath, the very simplicity of the purification *mikveh* seemed to shame the sensuous luxury of its pagan counterpart. If one bath was strictly for the pleasures of this world, the other was strikingly otherworldly.

Excellent examples of *mikvehs* can also be seen by visitors to the Wohl Museum in the Jewish Quarter of Jerusalem. There, in the wonderfully preserved ruins of a palatial first-century house, one can see at least two *mikvehs*. Jewish houses often had more than one of these ceremonial "baptisteries," used by women at least once a month and by men perhaps each morning. In some of the homes the *mikveh* would be located at the entrance to the house, so that anyone entering the house could purify himself from any possible uncleanness, such as dead animals or diseased persons in the marketplace.

Is it any wonder, then, that when Peter and the other apostles told the Jews on Pentecost to repent and be baptized, no one had to stop and ask what being baptized meant? It was the same kind of ritual immersion that the Jews were already performing day in and day out, albeit with three major differences.

Since, as Peter said, it was "for the forgiveness of your sins," they would need to do it only once, not continuously. Unlike ever before, it was also to be done "in the name of Jesus Christ," in recognition that only by his blood can anyone be washed clean. And—something no one under the Jewish purification laws would ever have dreamed possible—Peter promised that they would "receive the gift of the Holy Spirit."

Forgiveness of sins? The gift of the Holy Spirit? Now that's what I'd call a real *"mikveh"*!

The sad thing is that apparently the Essenes never accepted either the messiahship of Jesus or his once-for-all, saving *"mikveh"*. From the time of his death until theirs—a period of some 40 years— they continued to seek purification through their own repetitious ritual. Not faith, but works. Apparently not even John the Baptist (who some scholars have strained to link with the Essenes) had persuaded them to leave their ritual purification *mikvehs* and to accept, instead, his baptism of genuine, lasting repentance.

The problem with any ritual, of course, is that we too easily can go through the motions without having anything happen on the inside. That is as true of baptism into Christ as it was of the Essenes' *mikveh* ritual. Whether it's done once in a lifetime or five times a day, it's just too easy to take on a "been there, done that" attitude about spiritual purification. And that causes me to think long and hard about what my own *mikveh* has done for me lately.

If I read the writer of Hebrews correctly, there is supposed to be a crucial link between my outer cleansing and my inward cleansing. "Let us draw near to God with a sincere heart in full assurance of faith," says the writer, "having our hearts sprinkled to cleanse us from a guilty conscience and having our bodies washed with pure water."

If the body is to experience a cleansing *mikveh*, so too the heart. Neither purification without salvation nor salvation without purification can complete the picture. And that is where I begin to struggle. Though baptized into Christ, and trusting him for my salvation, I nevertheless know all too well the impurity of my own heart. Looking down into the *mikvehs* at Qumran, Masada, and Jerusalem, I was reminded of how little attention I have paid to purity in my own life.

I suppose that washing five times a day could be considered excessive legalism, or, worse yet, even obsessive-compulsive behavior. But, however far they may have missed the eagerly-awaited Messiah, I couldn't help but be convicted by the Essenes' commitment to purification. Would that I could stop whatever I'm doing five times a day and take a mental *mikveh*. To take inventory. To be honest with myself. To clean out the rubbish. To think on "whatsoever is pure."

My mind strays. My heart wanders. My soul gets lost. Maybe it's time I joined the young Bedouin shepherd boy and climbed to a higher plane in search of purity gone astray. Who knows what I might discover? By God's grace, it won't be just ancient scrolls in earthen jars, but the Living Word in a purer heart.

Purer in heart, O God, help me to be,
That I Thy holy face one day may see;
Keep me from secret sin,
Reign Thou my soul within;
Purer in heart help me to be.

—*Fannie E. Davison*

Chapter Eleven

"Consider

the generations

long past."

DEUTERONOMY 32:7

Heritage

It was a day of digs. Or "tels," to be exact—distinctive mounds where layers of ancient civilizations had been built on top of each other: Jericho, Hatzor, Dan, Megiddo. Unless you knew what you were looking for, you would have driven right by, never knowing what you were missing. But a closer look puts one into a time machine which, within just minutes, whirs you back centuries.

I've been to Jericho and its Tel e-Sultan several times, but I never fail to be amazed by the slice of life it reveals. Thanks particularly to archaeologist Kathleen Kenyon and her stratigraphic method of knifing deeply down through the strata rather than simply peeling back one layer after another, we can see evidence of civilizations reaching back to the eighth millennium B.C.

In fact, you can virtually count the civilizations for yourself. Just imagine slicing a wedge of a three-layered cake, removing the cut piece, and looking at the alternating layers of cake and filling. In some 45 feet of vertical debris at Tel e-Sultan, there are at least

20 easily discernible horizontal lines, indicating where one civilization was built upon the foundation of an earlier destroyed settlement on the same site. (White lines show stone rubble. Black charcoal lines tell us that this particular settlement was burned to the ground.)

Layer upon layer. Generation upon generation. The story of the tels is the story of civilization.

It should not have been surprising, then, that our day would have ended at another "tel" of sorts—Capernaum. At Capernaum there is no mound, and there are only one or two noticeable horizontal lines to suggest succeeding civilizations. Nevertheless, what I saw there prompted me, like never before, to think about my own spiritual foundations.

Capernaum, of course, was Jesus' home away from Nazareth, and the heart of Jesus' Galilean ministry. He spent some two years in residence there, teaching and performing miracles. Situated on the northern shore of the Sea of Galilee, Capernaum was the home of two sets of fishing brothers whom Jesus called to be apostles: Peter and Andrew, and James and John, the sons of Zebedee.

One of the most impressive of Jesus' miracles performed in Capernaum was the healing—at a distance—of the Roman centurion's servant. The centurion had enlisted the help of the local Jewish elders to approach Jesus on his behalf. When the elders came to Jesus with the centurion's request, they implored Jesus to honor the centurion's request. "This man deserves to have you do this," they said, "because he loves our nation and has built our synagogue."

Imagine my excitement, then, at being able to visit what apparently is the site of the very synagogue which the centurion had helped to build. On that site one can see not only the clearly recognizable foundations of the first-century synagogue but also the extensive ruins of a later synagogue from the second or perhaps the fourth century.

Virtually adjacent to the synagogue is another much-visited pilgrim site in Capernaum. In recent years a modern Franciscan church has been erected over the traditional site of Peter's house—perhaps the home where Jesus healed Peter's mother-in-law of her fever. The new church itself is built over the remains of a fifth-century octagonal church dedicated to Peter's memory.

Layer upon layer. Generation upon generation. Life is a never-ending "tel."

Which brings me to the most important "tel" of the day. On the way out of the Franciscan grounds, I spotted a row of columns that had been taken from the second synagogue. On one of the columns is an Aramaic inscription dedicated to "Alpheus the son of Zebedah the son of John," who had contributed to the building of the synagogue.

Speculative though it may be, it is altogether possible that there is profound significance in the names "John" and "Zebedah." Given the location (Capernaum) and the fact that family names were passed down for generations, these men may have been descendants of the apostle John, the son of Zebedee—possibly three centuries from the time of Christ. Possibly they were still believers. Possibly members of a synagogue of Messianic Jews dedicated to the cause of Christ. If so, what a heritage! If so, what a "tel!"

I confess that it's one of those times when I *want* to believe something happened the way I envision it. Just as there have been successive generations of Jews over the centuries, and successive generations of Gentile Christians, why could there not have been successive generations of Jewish Christians?

In fact, we know of at least three such generations in the case of Timothy, "whose mother was a Jewess and a believer." Add Timothy's grandmother to that list as well. In his second letter to Timothy the apostle Paul spoke with admiration of Timothy's faith, "which first lived in your grandmother Lois and in your mother Eunice and, I am persuaded, now lives in you also."

When faith is handed down from parent to child for generations, there is a kind of spiritual archaeology at work: layer upon layer, generation upon generation. Seen in the light of one of the stratigraphic digs, the foundations of faith often run far deeper than we think.

If, for some, faith is "first-generation" belief, for many more of us, our faith is built squarely upon the faith of those who have gone before. Or, as the hymn puts it so wonderfully: "Faith of our fathers, living still."

When I think of "faith" and "fathers," I don't have to look far afield. My own spiritual heritage on my father's side goes back to at least four generations of gospel preachers and teachers. I recently read with delight a brief autobiography by my great-great-grandfather, Valentine I. Stirman, who recounted that, in the years following the Civil War, he was a circuit-riding preacher in Texas. His son, Rolin R. Stirman, also preached; and Rolin's daughter (my grandmother, Eva Mae Smith) taught Sunday school and, as a young widow, raised five boys in the faith.

Following in the steps of his grandfather and great-grandfather, my own father, Frank L. Smith, was a gospel preacher from the age of 16 until the day he died. On that day, I had the distinct feeling that a torch was being passed along for me to carry.

Nor does even that rich spiritual heritage begin to cover the foundations upon which I have tried to build. There is also my mother's great faith, and her parents', and theirs. And the faith of aunts and uncles, and older cousins, and teachers too numerous to count. And then there are the unnamed, unknown persons of faith who influenced them, and the countless generations of faith even further removed.

Once a person begins to dig down through generations of faith, the layers seem to never end. Some of the believers in our supporting strata we will never know by name—hymnwriters, scholars, translators, reformers, and—lest we forget—untold martyrs, whose broken and burnt bodies appear as courageous "black lines" in the debris of civilizations past.

For the Christian, of course, a dig down through the ages ultimately brings one back to Capernaum and the first century, to a faith "built on the foundation of the apostles and prophets, with Christ Jesus himself as the chief cornerstone." If that heritage of faith doesn't stir one to pick up the torch and run with it, nothing will!

It gives me pause to think I could so easily have driven past Jericho, Hatzor, and Capernaum without realizing how much history I was missing. In this fast-paced world, it's often only the *here* and *now* that count, not the *there* and *then*.

But the time will come when I am as much a part of the on-going "tel" of this life as are those who have already gone before. So I'm beginning to think in different terms—not so much of *history* but of *heritage*.

To future generations, what will the "tel" of my life reveal? What kind of a foundation am I leaving for others to build on?

God grant me vision not just for tomorrow but for the ages to come.

> *Ask the former generations and find out what*
> *their fathers learned,*
> *for we were born only yesterday and know nothing,*
> *and our days on earth are but a shadow.*
> *Will they not instruct you and tell you?*
> *Will they not bring forth words from their*
> *understanding?*
>
> *—Job*

Chapter Twelve

"God . . . gave us

the ministry

of reconciliation."

2 CORINTHIANS 5:18

Reconciliation

We had driven all day when we found ourselves in Metulla, the northernmost town in Israel. I was intrigued by the road signs which pointed ahead to "The Good Fence." "What could 'The Good Fence' possibly be?" I wondered.

As the highway ended and we drove onto a rough, graveled road running through what looked like abandoned buildings on either side, it soon became clear that we had just run out of country. Depending upon how you look at it, we were either in southern Lebanon or smack in the middle of the Security Zone which had been created by Israel as a buffer against its northern neighbor.

There, just ahead of us, was "The Good Fence," the artificial military border, if not the official political one, between Israel and Lebanon. We all got out of the van and walked as far toward the fence as we dared. Keenly conscious of watching eyes, we ventured quick photos to provide proof of our presence, then hurried out of there!

Afterward it seemed a tame enough venture even in a country perpetually on a military alert. But within a week the very spot where we had been standing became center stage to a rocket-and-artillery battle between Israel and Lebanon!

In retrospect, it had been a day for fences. Traveling northward from Jericho to Bet-She'an, we had driven for miles alongside a high fence guarded by electronic sensors, cameras, and a special track for inspection by military vehicles. At a distance of perhaps one to three miles from the shoreline, the fence paralleled the Jordan River, which is the official boundary between Israel and its neighboring state of Jordan. Stern warnings affixed to the fence marked the territory behind the fence as a military no-go area.

Whether "good" fences or "bad" fences, Israel is a land of fences. And they're not particularly pretty, nor particularly comforting. It was like a breath of fresh air, then, when later that same day we headed up into the hills west of the Sea of Galilee to visit a Messianic Jewish couple in my friend Joseph's far-flung congregation. As we drove up to the house, we were greeted by friendly dogs, but thankfully no fences!

Like so many people in Israel today, Barry and Dalia are immigrants. They both came from the States—he, a computer whiz and management consultant; she, an artist and gracious hostess. As we sat around the table drinking tea and getting acquainted, my eye was continually drawn to the lovely flowers at the back of the house. After awhile I could no longer resist a closer view. Excusing myself, I took a walk out back and was captivated by the color and artistry of Dalia's garden.

What struck me most was the backdrop—a wall of tall, gorgeous cactus. I'm not sure why, but I hadn't expected to see cactus in Israel. But here it was, forming just the right frame for the fragrant roses and deep-red bougainvillea. Spectacular!

Back inside, I conveyed my "oohs" and "ahs" to Dalia for her beautiful garden. Then I asked her about the row of cactus. "Oh," she said, "that's my cactus fence."

"Cactus fence?"

In an instant the thought struck me that fences do indeed come in all sorts of packages. They needn't be barbed wire. They can even be cactus, prickly but beautiful. Where some fences snarl, other fences invite.

The next day, as we drove back to Jerusalem and stopped at a military checkpoint along the road, it occurred to me yet again that we were passing through a "fence." If you don't have the right papers, you can't get through. Checkpoints are as much fences as barbed wire and land mines.

And sometimes rivers as well, as in the case of the Jordan. In fact, the Jordan has been a "border fence" from ancient times, even between some of the tribes of Israel. At one point the Reubenites and Gadites (whose inheritance was east of the Jordan) were fearful that the day would come when the rest of the tribes of Israel would say, "The LORD has made the Jordan a boundary between us and you—you Reubenites and Gadites! You have no share in the LORD." Nobody likes to be fenced out.

There is nothing particularly wrong with boundaries, of course. God himself fixed a boundary between light and darkness, and between the ocean and the land. "I made the sand a boundary for the sea, an everlasting barrier it cannot cross."

What's more, God so honors territorial integrity that he repeatedly instructed the Israelites not to move ancient boundary markers. "Cursed is the man who moves his neighbor's boundary stone," said Jehovah. How much more blunt could he have been? And, by implication, comes this corollary: "Thou shalt not erect a fence *beyond* your own boundary line."

In that regard, I find it intriguing that Israel today has built "The Good Fence" between itself and Lebanon, not on the recognized border, but deeper into Lebanon territory. They call the newly created area a "security zone." Politics, and perhaps military wisdom aside, it is altogether fascinating how much "The Good Fence" is like the Mishnah, or oral law of the Jews. The rules of the Mishnah are extensions of scriptural commands. The idea of the rabbis was to "make a fence for the Torah"—that is, to make a fence around the Scriptures—so that there would be no chance of ever getting close enough to commit a violation. Call it a theological "security zone." In the eyes of the rabbis, the Mishnah is "The Good Fence."

Although the Mishnah was not formally compiled until the end of the second century A.D., it was this very process of "fence-building" which time and again drew Jesus' rebuke. Instead of enforcing God's boundaries for proper ritual and practice, the rabbis were enforcing their own boundaries. Good motives notwithstanding, they had moved the divine boundary stones and deprived the people of legitimate latitude which they should have been permitted to exercise.

The more I read the Gospels, the more I'm impressed with the number of fences Jesus came to tear down. Not only the "good fences" which, in our doctrinal insecurity, we erect as "security zones," but also the more personal fences of prejudice and discrimination which only breed distrust and hostility.

It is those personal fences that I've begun to look at more closely in my own life. If pressed, I would deny that I fence out anyone on the basis of race, or language, or social class. But I can't honestly say that I haven't built some "good fences" in the direction of certain other people, just to give myself a bit of a "comfort zone."

Look where I live. It's a long way from the inner city. Look where I shop. It's not exactly The Dollar Store. Look where I worship. Everyone there looks a lot like me. As the psalmist said, "The boundary lines have fallen for me in pleasant places."

So can I really say that I haven't moved some boundary stones, pushing my less-welcome neighbors further away? And have I not thereby robbed them of their dignity and created unnecessary distrust and hostility?

I know I'm taking a passage out of context to say so (the reference is to a wall between Jews and Gentiles), but when I think of how Jesus tore down fences, I'm sure he wants me to do the same. "For he himself is our peace, who has made the two one and has destroyed the barrier, the dividing wall of hostility. . . ." Jesus' ministry was not about fences and separation, but about broken barriers and reconciliation. Can my ministry—indeed, my *life*, be anything less?

It's time I inspected my fences. Given the hostile proliferation of literal and figurative barbed wire in the world, may all my fences be beautiful cactus fences—and not an inch beyond their proper boundaries!

Chapter Thirteen

"Blessed are those . . .

who have set their hearts

on pilgrimage."

PSALM 84:5

Pilgrimage

I've been down the Jericho Road, the road of the Good Samaritan, many times. It is the way not only to Jericho but north to the Galilee and south to the Dead Sea and Masada. From Jerusalem the drop-off is steep. In just three miles the road descends 3600 feet to below sea level.

On either side of the highway is the Judean desert, refreshingly green and graced with wild flowers in the springtime, but typically dry, hot, and dusty during the rest of the year. There, on the dry hillsides, you will see small herds of goats being shepherded by Bedouins. Considering the harsh terrain, one wonders what the goats find to feed on. Which tells the tale of the Bedouins: They are constantly on the move in search of food and water for their flocks. For traditional Bedouins, little has changed since Abraham lived the life of a nomadic pastoralist.

Yet something isn't quite right about those Bedouins along the Jericho Road. They don't seem to move—ever. Even when my visits to Israel have come years apart, I have seen the same bedouin tents in the exact same spot. Further suspicion is aroused by the tents themselves, which, instead of being made from the traditional goatskins, are obviously made from some synthetic material; or perhaps it's the corrugated metal fencing around the stalls for the goats, or the Mercedes parked nearby, or the recently erected satellite dish.

But somehow I suspect that this particular Bedouin camp is strictly for tourists, complete with the mandatory "photo ops" and camel rides. This is unfortunate, because the Bedouin culture in the Middle East has a rich and vibrant history, only now being decimated by modern urbanization. (Today Bedouins even have their own cities, mostly in the Gaza and the Negev, complete with houses, streets, and shopping markets.)

The time was when Bedouins would have chafed at the very thought of giving up their seasonal migrations. From time immemorial they have had legal "wandering rights." After all, wandering has been their livelihood, their lifestyle—indeed, their very lives.

Today, as I drove past the Bedouins on the Jericho Road, I noticed hundreds of storks circling over the same Judean hills. I was struck by the thought that true Bedouins are perhaps more in tune with nature than the rest of us. When I asked about the storks, I was told they were migrating from Scandinavia down to Africa. Now *that's* some wandering!

Centuries ago the storks must also have captured Jeremiah's attention. "Even the stork in the sky knows her appointed seasons," he wrote, "and the dove, the swift and the thrush observe the time of their migration."

Wandering. Migration. Pilgrimage. The words seemed to flow together in a natural sequence. I had just left Jerusalem during the time of Passover, which for Jews is a pilgrimage feast and for Christians a pilgrimage in honor of Christ's death and resurrection.

Perhaps, then, we have more in common with the wandering Bedouins than might first appear. We too have seasonal migrations, if nothing more than trips home for Christmas and Thanksgiving. City-bound though we may be, in all of us is a bit of the Bedouin. If only in heart, we are all wanderers, we are all pilgrims.

When I think of pilgrims, I think of those who are in search not of food and water for their flocks but of spiritual nourishment for their souls. The Queen of Sheba, for example, traveled great distances to drink from Solomon's wisdom. And the magi followed the star at the time of Jesus' birth. Despite being wise men themselves (or indeed *because* they were wise), they came seeking Jesus.

Whether already wise, or perhaps *seeking* wisdom, the godly pilgrim is but a spiritual Bedouin.

One of my favorite hymns, written in 1865 by I. N. Carman, suggests a grand view of pilgrimage:

> *Here we are but straying pilgrims;*
> *Here our path is often dim;*
> *But to cheer us on our journey,*
> *Still we sing this wayside hymn:*

> *Yonder over the rolling river,*
> *Where the shining mansions rise,*
> *Soon will be our home forever,*
> *And the smile of the blessed Giver*
> *Gladdens all our longing eyes.*

Compared with the heavenly home to come, our life on earth is merely a pilgrimage. A stop along the way. A present wandering. A migration for a season.

Sometimes, of course, spiritual wandering is caused not by seeking but by *sin*. For example, Cain, the archetypical sinner, was told by God that he would be "a restless wanderer on the earth." And, of course, the sinful Israelites wandered in the wilderness for 40 years before God permitted them to enter the Promised Land.

But wholly apart from sin, the Bible presents this life as a pilgrimage in a foreign land. As Albert Brumley put it to music:

> *This world is not my home, I'm just a*
> *passing thru',*
> *My treasures are laid up somewhere*
> *beyond the blue;*
> *The angels beckon me from heaven's*
> *open door,*
> *And I can't feel at home in this world*
> *anymore.*

Seen in that light, I love the way in which Jacob described his age to Pharaoh: "The years of my pilgrimage are a hundred and thirty. My years have been few and difficult, and they do not equal the years of the pilgrimage of my fathers." Whether 21, 40, or 75, we are never "over the hill," just a bit further along on our pilgrimage!

Thinking of my brief life as a pilgrimage provides an altogether different perspective on my earthly citizenship: I was never meant to be a permanent resident—only a resident alien!

In that great roll call of faith in Hebrews chapter 11, the men and women of old who were honored for their faith were all characterized by one thing: "They admitted that they were aliens and strangers on earth." The writer of Hebrews goes on to explain that "people who say such things show that they are looking for a country of their own. If they had been thinking of the country they had left, they would have had opportunity to return. Instead, they were longing for a better country—a heavenly one. Therefore God is not ashamed to be called their God, for he has prepared a city for them."

We will not always be spiritual Bedouins, for God has prepared a heavenly city and a mansion for eternity. But for as long as we are on this earth, we lose a crucial sense of orientation if we ever forget that we are merely pilgrims in search of our true home.

Through Jeremiah, God lamented that his people wandered away and "forgot their own resting place." Have you and I forgotten our true resting place, our true home? Do we live our lives frenetically moving about from one insignificant activity to the next as if this life is all there is? As God's elect, says the apostle Peter, "we are strangers in the world." So, "live your lives as strangers here."

Whether Bedouin, stork, or pilgrim, "wandering rights" never give one cause for an aimless existence. Bedouins wander for a purpose; storks always have a compass setting; and pilgrims keep their eyes on the goal.

I have to confess that I haven't always thought of myself as a pilgrim on earth. In my younger years, particularly, I was more of a tourist. I wandered all over the earth, but it was rarely a spiritual pilgrimage.

As merely a tourist on my first visit to Israel, my heart was never in it. No, my *soul* was never in it! And so I missed the whole point of being there. I missed the moment; I missed the message; I missed the meaning.

Since then I haven't returned as a tourist, but as a pilgrim. And what I have encountered has been a whole different world. Which causes me to think more seriously about my spiritual journey on this terrestrial ball. How shall I spend the rest of my life? As a tourist on a flying stopover, or as a pilgrim on a holy quest?

Chapter Fourteen

"I die

every day."

1 CORINTHIANS 15:31

Sacrifice

I still have mixed feelings about Masada. Situated 1400 feet above the Dead Sea, surrounded on all sides by cliffs, and bordered by the harsh Wilderness of Judea, Masada seems impregnable. Of course, that was the whole idea.

Upon his return from Rome in 37 B.C. as King of Judea, Herod began construction on his royal sanctuary and fortress on Masada's tablelike summit. In addition to massive fortifications, there were elaborate palaces, and enough storehouses and cisterns to withstand a protracted war. Some 50 years later, that very impregnability would backfire on the Romans who succeeded Herod after his death.

With Herod's departure, only a small garrison was stationed at Masada, leaving it vulnerable despite the fortifications. Having become a soft target, it easily fell in A.D. 66 to Jewish zealots. Four years later the zealots were joined by survivors of the fall of Jerusalem, setting the stage for the famous confrontation between the 960 defenders of Masada and the 10,000-man-strong Tenth Legion.

Today one has the choice of ascending Masada on foot by way of a winding, tortuous path or by taking a breathtaking ride in a cable car. No stranger to ease wherever I can find it, I chose the latter mode. On the ascent, I could see below me the restored walls of one of the Roman camps, from where Flavius Silva, the Roman general, laid siege to the fortress in the spring of A.D. 73. Using Jewish slaves, the general's engineers built a quite remarkable earthen ramp up the western side of Masada, sufficient to support a mobile siege tower, complete with catapults, arrow launchers, and a giant battering ram.

Stepping out of the cable car and surveying the bleak scenery in every direction, I was sure that neither side in the confrontation had much at stake in either holding or conquering Masada, other than sheer principle. The Romans might have said that they needed to wipe out the last pocket of Jewish resistance, but here they already had the troublemakers trapped. It was probably the insult of Jews occupying any part of Roman territory that drew the Romans' ire.

For the Jewish defenders, it could only have been a matter of principle, given the acknowledged fact that they had no chance whatever to defeat the Roman Legion. In fact, it was that very principle—freedom over slavery—which ultimately led to one of the most revered moments in Jewish history. And, for me, one of the most troubling.

When at last the day came that the Romans were ready to ascend the ramp and commence the long-awaited assault, they set fire to the fortress and battered their way inside. But the soldiers, anticipating a bloody fight with the well-armed zealots, were greeted with only an eerie silence. What they discovered still brings chills to anyone who stands in the middle of Masada and looks around trying to imagine that historic day. Purposely and methodically, the 960 defenders of Masada—men, women, and children—had committed mass suicide.

It still brings chills, but also misgivings. I can't help but think of a number of modern-day mass suicides by other religious zealots. If I have disapproved of their actions (as I have), why should I be stirred by the patriotic fervor of the Masada defenders?

Through the pen of Jewish historian Josephus Flavius, we have an account of the moving Elazar oration which proposed the suicide pact. (His speech may have been relayed to Josephus by one of the two women and three children who survived.) On the surface, there is much that rings true.

> *Let us at once choose death with honor and do the kindest thing we can for ourselves, our wives and children, while it is still possible to show ourselves any kindness. After all, we were born to die, we and those we brought into the world; this even the luckiest must face.*
>
> *But outrage, slavery, and the sight of our wives led away to shame with our children—these are not evils to which man is subject by the laws of nature. . . .*
>
> *Let us die unenslaved by our enemies, and leave this world as free men in company with our wives and children.*

What decision would I have made under those circumstances? Would it have made any difference if I knew that survival meant inevitable torture for myself and the rape of my wife? Would I suffer less if death came by my own hand? Would my suicide convey some important message or defend some inviolable principle?

At least some of these questions are the very ones being asked regarding euthanasia for the terminally ill—questions which seem to disregard God's sovereignty over my life and its ending. "Death before slavery" is one thing; suicide, quite another. (Not even Patrick Henry's purported challenge, "Give me liberty or give me death," contemplated death by his own hand.)

You need only contrast the infamous suicide of Judas with the noble and courageous death of Jesus to appreciate the fact that suicide is not God's way, not even when the most important principle possible—spiritual freedom before spiritual slavery—is at stake. If we learn anything at all from the manner of Jesus' death, surely it is that meekly submitting to a death one does not choose is not the same as personally exercising that option. And, given the excruciating pain of crucifixion, who would have had better cause to "end it quickly"? Yet, for Jesus, there was but one response: "Not my will, but thine."

Why then should I have mixed feelings at all about the self-inflicted deaths of Masada's defenders? Why not simply get on the first cable car down the mountain in silent protest of their mass suicide? Why instead the lingering feeling of being stirred by their tragically misguided bravery?

I'll tell you what I think it is. It's the stirring feeling that these Jewish zealots believed in something so strongly that they were willing to die for it. For the moment, forget *how* they died. Merely consider *why* they died.

Standing in the middle of Masada's ruins and trying as best I could to imagine the unimaginable, I found myself asking one of the most important questions any of us could ever ask: *What would I be willing to die for?*

What immediately comes to mind, of course, are the lives of those with whom I have some special relation: my wife, my family, and my closest friends. If it should ever come down to one of their lives or mine, I would like to think I would step forward and do the right thing. At such times, surely love acts instinctively.

I confess I am less certain about dying "for King and country." Not that I lack patriotism or think that I am somehow above losing my life in some distant foxhole. Nor do I lack appreciation for those who gave their "last full measure" so that I might enjoy the freedoms which could only be bought at the price of too much spilt blood. It's just that, as a Christian, I find the whole notion of war extremely complicated. Even if I myself would be willing to *die* on the field of battle, under what circumstances would I be willing to *kill* on the field of battle?

The thought of being martyred for Christ brings me back to greater certainty—at least hypothetically. Not facing any immediate possibility of being fed to the lions or facing a firing squad because of my faith, it is perhaps too easy to say that I would be willing to die, but I certainly hope I would have the strength to honor Christ as he has honored you and me.

And honor us he has! As we are reminded by the apostle Paul, "Very rarely will anyone die for a righteous man, though for a good man someone might possibly dare to die. But God demonstrates his own love for us in this: While we were still sinners, Christ died for us." That which motivated Jesus to lay down his life for us was anything but instinctual. In human terms, his death made no sense. We were not the lovable, but the unlovable. We were not family, but strangers and aliens. We were not righteous and worthy, but sinful and unworthy. Yet, still, he laid down his life for us!

So, knowing that martyrdom is but the remotest possibility and believing that suicide even in the defense of principle is not God's way, perhaps the question is not, What I would *die for?* but rather, What would I be willing to *lay down my life for?*

Put this way, the question is no longer hypothetical. I'm no longer off the hook. When Jesus said, "Greater love has no one than this, that he lay down his life for his friends," he wasn't talking about my taking a bullet intended for someone else, or committing mass suicide to make a crucial statement about the importance of freedom. In fact, he wasn't talking about *dying* at all, but rather *living*.

Jesus died to teach us how to live.

What then does it mean to live like Jesus died? It means to give the "last full measure," not of our blood, but of our selves. It means learning to love as Jesus loved. "This is how we know what love is: Jesus Christ laid down his life for us. And we ought to lay down our lives for our brothers." Together with Paul, "I eagerly expect and hope that I will . . . have sufficient courage so that now as always Christ will be exalted in my body, *whether by life or by death*."

When I begin to think of my willingness to "lay down my life" in terms of loving and serving others, I am drawn inexorably back to Masada and to the 960 defenders who chose death over slavery. What a waste of human potential! Even as slaves, they would have had much to live for—just as other Jewish slaves before them. Especially the children.

Who knows? Among the children might have been another Moses, to lead them out of captivity. Among them might have been another Joshua, to lead them into a land of peace and promise. Solomon was right in saying, "Anyone who is among the living has hope—even a live dog is better than a dead lion!" And where there is hope, one can lay down his life and keep it at the same time.

For that reason I disagree with what the zealots did at Masada. Still, I am deeply in their debt for forcing me to ask a question I too often ignore: What would I be willing to die for? Unless we know what we're willing to die for, how shall we know what we're willing to live for?

Chapter Fifteen

"Whoever follows me

will never walk in darkness."

JOHN 8:12

Vision

At the time it had seemed like a good idea. But all of a sudden a draft of air blew out all three candles, and we were enshrouded in darkness—right in the middle of Hezekiah's Tunnel. Right in the middle of the Arab village where, only two days before, our van had been pelted with rocks by tough young boys, displeased at nothing more than seeing the wrong kind of license plate in their territory. And now Ruth and I were at the mercy of a young man from the same neighborhood whom we had met only minutes earlier as we walked down the steep hill from the Dung Gate toward the old City of David and the Pool of Siloam.

One match, two matches, and then three failed to light our candles. I wondered just how many more matches Nihad had in his little box. The knee-high water was just cold enough to add to the apprehension, not to mention the fact that the walls on either side of us were only two to three feet wide and some five to six feet high. I started calculating what it would take to make our way out of the tunnel in total darkness.

After several tense moments, one of the candles caught flame, and we ever so carefully shared that flame with the other two. The renewed light from the candles dispelled both the darkness around us and a growing anxiety.

It was one of those times when you ask yourself, "What in the world have I gotten myself into? Why am I doing this?" I have to admit that it was partly the sheer sense of adventure that had attracted us, not unlike Indiana Jones in "Raiders of the Lost Ark." The risk represented by the earlier stoning incident and friends' stories of dead tarantulas floating in the water only heightened the adventure!

But mostly we had come to touch a part of ancient history. In a land of holy places largely obscured by the passage of time, the actual sites of tombs and temples are frustratingly speculative. By contrast, this tunnel, built in 701 B.C. by King Hezekiah of Judah, is rock-solid evidence that the biblical accounts of that period are accurate in every detail.

Designed to be a conduit from the Spring of Gihon (then outside the city walls) to the Pool of Siloam, the S-shaped tunnel is some 1750 feet long. Even in the dim light of three small candles, we could appreciate the ingenuity of the scheme—especially knowing that two separate teams of workers had begun at opposite ends of the tunnel, working their way toward each other. Although the separate tunnels were off center by a scarce 12 inches in elevation, we could see evidence of some confusion where the workers had to merge their respective tunnels using nothing more scientific than the sounds of each other's pickaxes.

After slowly making our way through the uneven tunnel for some 20 minutes, I noticed that Nihad's candle had gone out once again. It had melted down to the point where he could no longer hold it. When I offered to give him mine, he said, "No, we are near the pool." I must admit that those words sounded pretty good to me.

By that time the bottoms of my rolled-up trousers were thoroughly soaked, and my back and neck were sore from constantly leaning over to avoid hitting my head. A few more curves, a few more steps, and I began to sense the proverbial "light at the end of the tunnel." One last turn, and there it was in the distance—sunshine pouring into the opening leading from the tunnel to the Pool of Siloam.

At last, we had made it! I blew out my candle, bid farewell to the darkness, and stepped into the light.

Hezekiah's Tunnel had more than lived up to its billing, but the Pool of Siloam was, for me, a disappointment. Having seen the great Pool of Bethesda, I was expecting something far more grandiose than a shallow pool only 15 by 50 feet. Unfortunately, because of alterations over the centuries, there is no way to know its original size, nor its size at the time that Jesus had the blind man go to this pool and wash off the mud that Jesus had put over his eyes. Remember the blind man?

I am certain that, unlike me, when the man blind from birth got his first glimpse of the Pool of Siloam, there is not a chance in the world that he was disappointed! It was he who first gave us those wonderful, familiar words which we now sing about God's amazing grace: "I was blind, but now I see!"

"But what did he see?" As I sat in the middle of the pool on what seemed to be the base of one of the original columns, I tried to imagine the very first images that might have come to his startled eyes. There would have been the pool, of course, with its columns rising to the height of the portico. Surely, too, he would have seen the other bathers, themselves undoubtedly surprised at his miraculous healing. And if that day was anything like our day at the pool, he surely must have looked up to a brilliant blue sky with dumbfounded amazement!

The text tells us that immediately after his healing, the man "came home seeing." Can you imagine what it must be like to see your parents for the very first time? And perhaps brothers and sisters, and aunts and uncles, and your neighbors and friends whom you've heard and touched for a lifetime, but never actually seen?

The mind races. Surely there must have been surprises—even disappointments—as he saw, not the images he had formed in his mind over the years, but the actual appearances of those closest to him. Was his mother as pretty as he had always thought she was? Was his father of the stature and bearing that the tone of his voice might have suggested? Did they look older or younger than he had imagined?

Yet it was what he saw later in the day—the face of the One who had healed him—that pushes me beyond the line of curiosity to sheer envy. How I would love to have lived when he lived and to have looked into the very eyes of Jesus! Surely that alone would have been worth a lifetime of blindness.

Then again, I wonder if I've romanticized Jesus' physical appearance to the point where I might actually be disappointed if I could see Jesus' face. The Pharisees weren't the least bit impressed with Jesus. For them, Jesus was just another blasphemous messianic pretender—a "Sabbath sinner" who somehow managed to trick people into thinking they were healed. Apparently nothing about Jesus' physical appearance had any special convincing qualities.

This observation is underscored by the fact that the man who had been healed of his blindness tells us nothing about Jesus' physical appearance. What he shares with us about Jesus did not come from his gift of *sight* but from his even more precious gift of spiritual *insight*. When asked who had healed him, the man had 20/20 spiritual vision, saying simply, "He is a prophet." Who but a man of God (or indeed the Son of God!) could open the eyes of the blind?

With Jesus, one might be expected to "just know" that—at the very least—he was a prophet. But did the man's new spiritual insight carry over to other, less-obvious judgments? Did he, for example, have a new sense about people in general: their character, their nature, their innermost selves? Looking back on my own experience at the Pool of Siloam, I have begun to realize more than ever before what a great difference there is between sight and insight.

Remember my apprehension about Nihad, who had offered his services to guide us through Hezekiah's Tunnel? I confess that what I had first seen was just another young Arab "terrorist," like the ones who had earlier thrown stones at our van. Could we trust him? Was it safe to follow a complete stranger through a dark tunnel? Was he leading us into some trap where I would emerge from the tunnel with one less billfold than I entered with?

Once I was safely through the tunnel, billfold intact, all I saw was a friendly, enterprising young Arab who was earning a few extra shekels by providing a legitimate service to passing tourists. My generous tip silently apologized for having first misjudged him. Preconceptions had blurred my vision of Nihad.

Surely the same type of prejudging also explains the earlier stoning. The young toughs who pelted our van undoubtedly assumed from our license plate that we were local Jews, not tourists from America. They could hardly have known how much sympathy we have for the plight of Palestinians in Israel, pawns in a political war hardly of their choosing. We were not the enemies they assumed.

So now I'm beginning to wonder just how clear my perception of people really is. Am I seeing them clearly, by the objective light of day, or am I seeing them only in the distrustful darkness of some blurred preconception?

When it comes to perceiving the good and the bad in others, which is my greater vision: sight or insight?

Looking at people only externally—by their physical appearance, or perhaps by their job status, bank account, or degree of education—is tunnel vision, easily misleading, easily wrong. By contrast, I keep thinking that having true insight into a person is a lot like what happens when all the candles blow out in a darkened tunnel. At first there is nothing but total, blinding darkness. Yet before long your eyes begin to adjust to the darkness, and you can actually see more than you might ever have imagined.

If only I could have the patience to let the eyes of my heart adjust to the darkness of others' souls! Not simply to rely upon sight, but to seek insight. Not simply to rely upon my own vision, but to seek after God's. Perhaps then, by seeing others more clearly, my own blindness might be washed away. Perhaps then, too, I might catch a glimpse of that wondrous face I've so longed to see—the face of him whose love is reflected in the eyes of every soul that has ever needed healing.

So touch me and wash me, Lord, in the cleansing pool of your divine insight. "Open my eyes, Lord. I want to see Jesus."

Open my eyes, that I may see
Glimpses of truth Thou hast for me;
Place in my hands the wonderful key
That shall unclasp and set me free.

Silently now I wait for Thee,
Ready, my God, Thy will to see;
Open my eyes, illumine me,
Savior Divine!

—Clara H. Scott

Chapter Sixteen

"The battle

is the LORD'S."

1 SAMUEL 17:47

Struggle

I stood on the easternmost edge of the tel at Megiddo and looked slightly north across the Plain of Esdraelon toward Mount Tabor. Then I turned to look south and east toward Mount Gilboa and the Jezreel Valley. As if viewing history on a wide screen, I could see in my mind's eye scores of famous Old Testament battles that took place in this ancient crossroads of civilization.

One battle that stands out pitted Barak against Sisera. Shamed by Deborah, Barak had swooped down from Mount Tabor to fight the Canaanites. If you look intently enough, you can almost see Sisera's 900 iron chariots and all his men being routed by Barak's foot soldiers. (But of course it was left to a woman, Jael, to drive the tent peg through Sisera's temple!)

Then there was the battle between Israel's King Jehu and Ahaziah, king of Judah. The text says that, after being mortally wounded, Ahaziah "escaped to Megiddo and died there."

And there was the battle which probably never should have taken place. While Josiah was king, Pharaoh Neco of Egypt went up

---

to Carchemish to help the king of Assyria. Showing more bravery than good sense, King Josiah marched out to engage him. When Neco made a genuine attempt to avoid battle, Josiah disguised himself, "went to fight him on the plain of Megiddo," and ended up getting himself killed by Neco's archers.

Strategically located at the intersection of the arterial roads of antiquity, Megiddo guarded the vital Eeron Pass along what the Romans called the Via Maris, or Highway of the Sea. (My underpowered rental car huffed and puffed to climb up over the narrow pass.) It was that road which connected Egypt in the south with Assyria and Mesopotamia in the north and east.

Whenever Egypt wanted to go north, or Assyria wanted to come south, you could count on trouble along the way. For that reason King Solomon made Megiddo one of his "chariot cities," as did King Ahab, who, like Hezekiah, also constructed an ingenious water supply, the tunnel of which you can still walk through today. In fact, excavations reveal some 25 different levels of occupation, going back to 3500 B.C..

I sat down on a rock to rest and to reflect. In a way, Megiddo was symbolic of my own life. Like Megiddo, I too have found myself in a perennial state of struggle and inner conflict. Spiritual struggle. Spiritual conflict.

In fact, it did not escape me that my life was "layered" in much the same way as the tel at Megiddo, each layer representing different struggles I have faced over the years. Just when I have conquered one area of my life, I have been conquered by yet another. Or, put more positively, with each defeat I have rebounded to build upon that experience, even if I have later found myself having to rebuild all over again!

On that day, in that place, I couldn't help but think more deeply than ever about something that has always been curious to me. Why does the Old Testament have so many passages devoted to battles and war and fighting? Chapter after chapter, page after page, is filled with battle reports, as if from a war correspondent. After awhile you get the idea that Israel spent more time fighting than working or worshiping.

Perhaps God is trying to tell us that war is an unacceptable means of resolving conflict. And yet there were many times in the Old Testament when it was God himself who ordered Israel into battle, and even to kill women and children. For the most part, I've managed to accept that seeming inconsistency with the thought that God was teaching Israel the tough lesson of uncompromising obedience. Perhaps wiping out all possible potential for pagan influence was the only way. Still, I can't help but think there is something more I'm supposed to learn from the endless battles I read about.

Could it be that God is trying to show me how he regards my own struggles in the spiritual arena? I wonder if I'm not supposed to learn from Barak something about what it means to be a morally pure *man*. Remember, it took a morally conscious *woman* to remind Barak of his responsibilities before God. How many times as a man have I made it a woman's responsibility to draw the moral line?

I wonder, too, if I'm not supposed to learn something from King Ahaziah, who died in battle for little more reason than that he had chosen the wrong friends. He had gone out to fight King Jehu only because he happened to be hanging around with Joram, son of the wicked Jezebel. Could that have been part of my problem over the years—choosing the wrong friends? Have I so easily forgotten what Paul said about bad company corrupting good character?

And I suspect the lesson from King Josiah is all too obvious. He thought he had protected himself in battle by putting on a disguise. I've been there, too—going out into the world, trying to pretend I was someone other than who I am. The more I read the Scriptures, the more closely I identify with all the language of struggle and battle, especially when Peter talks about abstaining "from sinful desires, which war against your soul." There *is* a war going on, isn't there?

More times than I want to admit, I know exactly what Paul was talking about when he anguished, "I see another law at work in the members of my body, waging war against the law of my mind and making me a prisoner of the law of sin at work within my members."

Just when you think you have committed yourself to purity of thought and action, just when you think you've built yourself a mental Megiddo to guard that vital passage between you and the world—all of a sudden the enemy sneaks in and you're doing battle all over again.

Those are the times when I feel a certain kinship with the Reubenites and Gadites, of whom it was said, "They cried out to God during the battle. He answered their prayers, because they trusted in him." At those times my prayers have been the prayers of the psalmist: "All my enemies are before you." And again, "How long must I wrestle with my thoughts . . . ? How long will my enemy triumph over me?"

God knows the enemies I'm fighting. And he cares.

More than just caring, the good news is that, in all my battles, God is on my side! From the psalmist comes the assurance that "with God we will gain the victory, and he will trample down our enemies." If I have experienced defeat, praise God, I have also known victory!

In his wondrous Revelation, John sees a vision of God's ultimate judgment on mankind, which, through the use of the word *Armageddon*, he associates with the historic battleground of Megiddo. The scene he describes is a harvest of the earth, upon which God's wrath is imposed. With the pouring out of seven terrifying bowls comes a sense of climactic finality, in which God's righteousness and holiness are manifested through a cleansing of sin from the world.

Positioned at the center of this eternal conflict, Armageddon symbolizes all battles between Good and Evil—past, present, and future.

In the closing act of this section of Revelation, flashes of lightning, peals of thunder, an earthquake, and hundred-pound hailstones are followed by a loud voice from the heavenly throne, saying, "It is done!" One can hardly miss the obvious parallel between this scene and that awful hour of crucifixion when the whole of heaven and earth shook at Jesus' own words, "It is finished."

The message of Armageddon is the good news that the outcome of the battle between Good and Evil is no longer in doubt. Ours is the victory! Through the death of him who was slain for the sins of the world, both sin and death have been conquered—once and for all!

If that thought doesn't put a praise on your lips, nothing will. Yet the personal message of Armageddon has more to do with the battles which you and I will fight this very day than with the final battle at the end of time.

"Final" doesn't mean that the struggle is over, or that we don't have to keep fighting either the world from without or the enemy from within. It simply means that we need not give up hope, for the outcome is already assured. Good has already triumphed! Evil has already been defeated! Satan can't beat us!

On a rock at Megiddo, in the solitude of my thoughts, I sat at a table of peace—a table that had been specially prepared for me in the presence of all my enemies. And when my reverie was over, I put on my armor, took renewed courage, and launched out once again into the fray. But this time, walking closer than ever to the One who has already fought the greatest battle ever—and won!

> *O my God, I trust in Thee,*
> *Let me not be ashamed,*
> *Let not my enemies triumph over me.*

> —Charles Monroe

Chapter Seventeen

"Your hearts

must be fully committed

to the LORD."

1 KINGS 8:61

Allegiance

I couldn't help but wonder: Would Elijah have approved of the statue which has been erected in his honor at the Carmelite Monastery of Muhraqah? With a crooked sword raised menacingly above his head, and his foot pushing down on the shoulder of a grimacing prophet of Baal, Elijah looks fierce indeed! Give him another second, and the prophet of Baal's head will surely be dropping from the 15-foot base of the marble monument.

My guess is that Elijah might howl with laughter at the sculptor's rendition of his likeness. After all, there were no photos or sketches or models to work from, so the representation is all sheer conjecture and imagination. On the other hand, Elijah might not be at all pleased. From the little we know of him, there is nothing to suggest that he had a great sense of humor!

If anything, Elijah was a man of striking contradiction—both courageous and fearful; both extroverted and introverted; both strong and weak to the extreme. It was Elijah, you'll recall, who announced the famine that would come over the land of Israel because of its idolatry; who was fed meat and bread by the ravens while he hid out from the king; who performed the miracle of the widow's replenishing flour; and who raised that same widow's son from the dead.

If that's all we knew of Elijah, we might focus on how very similar his ministry and miracles were to those of Jesus. But in the aftermath of the miracle for which he is best known, we see Elijah cowering in a cave, feeling sorry for himself, and moaning to God about how he is the only righteous person left on earth! At that point the comparison with Jesus breaks down.

But we've rushed past the pinnacle of Elijah's prophetic mission, and the incident for which he is best remembered—the great contest with the prophets of Baal on Mount Carmel. It was Elijah who proposed the contest to King Ahab in order to prove Jehovah's superiority over the fertility god Baal. Ahab had introduced Baal worship in Israel and had set up a pagan Asherah pole in violation of God's strict prohibitions against idolatry.

The setting for the contest—on the slopes of Mount Carmel—could not have been more appropriate. From early Canaanite times, the hills in the area known as "Mount Carmel" (between the Mediterranean Sea and the Plain of Esdraelon) had been covered with shrines to Baal. Because Baal worship was persisting despite God's covenant with Israel, the time had come for a showdown. So Elijah invited Ahab to convene a great gathering of Israel at Mount Carmel, and to bring with him 450 prophets of Baal.

When the people and the pagan prophets were all assembled, Elijah challenged them, "How long will you waver between two opinions? If the LORD is God, follow him; but if Baal is God, follow him."

With that, Elijah proposed that two bulls be prepared for sacrifice on separate altars. Without setting the sacrifices alight, each side would call on its respective god to send down fire for the sacrifice. "The god who answers by fire—he is God." The prophets of Baal readily agreed to the contest and prepared their sacrifice.

From morning to noon they shouted to Baal and danced about wildly, but there was no fire. Elijah taunted them, saying, "Shout louder! Perhaps he is deep in thought, or busy, or traveling. Maybe he is sleeping and must be awakened." A literal translation, which most versions delicately avoid, gives you some flavor for Elijah's acerbic personality. What he actually suggested was that Baal may have fallen asleep while sitting on the toilet!

Naturally, that suggestion sent the prophets into a frenzy. For the remainder of the day they shouted louder and louder, and even cut themselves with swords and spears until they were a bloody mess. But "there was no response, no one answered, no one paid attention."

As evening approached, Elijah built an altar of 12 stones and prepared the sacrifice. To heighten the drama, he ordered that the altar be drenched three times with water until it was absolutely soaked. Then he prayed to God, and God sent down a ferocious fire which consumed the sacrifice—meat, wood, water, stones, dirt, and all! Amazed and convinced, the people fell prostrate and cried, "The LORD—he is God! The LORD—he is God!"

Who knows how long their renewed faith would remain steadfast? But when Elijah ordered them to seize the prophets of Baal and slaughter them, it wasn't long before blood was flowing in the Kishon River at the foot of Mount Carmel. All 450 were killed that day. Hence the statue of Elijah with sword held high.

Apart from the statue itself, and a replica altar made of 12 stones in the monastery's chapel, there is little to discover at the traditional site of the contest. When I arrived, the most noticeable excitement was found in the scores of picnics taking place all over the grounds of the monastery. It was the last day of Passover, and it seemed the whole of Israel had broken out their barbecues and headed for the hills. (The irony of the smoke and the smell of meat being grilled by fire did not escape me.)

After taking in a fabulous panoramic view from the monastery balcony, I got into my car and headed north along the ridge toward the town of Daliyat el Carmel, a popular Druze community. The Druze are an Arabic-speaking people with their own secret religion—a spinoff from Islam. Unlike the rest of Israel, the town was wide-open for business. In fact, it is well-known that many of the more secular Jews come to Daliyat el Carmel during Passover just to get the leavened bread that is available there. All along the roads I saw cars stopped at places where Druze women were baking large, thin pieces of bread—almost like a pizza—on what looked like an upside-down kettle. After shaping the dough, the women would place it on a kind of oversized round pillow, then slap the pillow down on top of the "kettle."

As I later walked through the town, I couldn't resist having a falafel (a kind of Middle East taco) made with the special Druze bread. Between bites I looked around me in the open-air cafe and was struck by another irony. Not unlike their Israelite predecessors who had turned to Baal worship, the Jews sitting all around me eating the bread forbidden during Passover were not real Jews. Not observing Jews. Not Jews by faith, only by birth. Of course, if I had turned to them and suggested that they were not real Jews, I'm virtually certain that I would have received a verbal barrage in return. Nevertheless, they would be hard-pressed to deny that their world is as secular as it is Jewish.

And that is when I'm sure I saw Elijah—sword raised high above his head—shouting to them, "How long will you waver between two opinions? Are you really a Jew, or just Jew-*ish?*"

The obvious implication came thundering home. It wasn't just the *Jews* that Elijah was shouting at. Another quick glance and I'm sure I saw Elijah—sword raised high above his head—shouting directly at me, "How long will you waver between two opinions? Are you really a Christian, or just Christian-*ish?*"

What could I possibly say in my own defense? Could I deny that my world, too, is an adulterated blend of the secular and the sacred? Do we not all have one foot in heaven and one foot in the world?

Oh, it's not to say that I have any doubts about my faith in God. I can honestly join Paul in saying, "I am not ashamed, because I know whom I have believed, and am convinced that he is able to guard what I have entrusted to him for that day." Nor would anyone who knows me well ever associate me with the kind of person described as being "blown here and there by every wind of teaching." My friends will be the first to tell you that I am often wrong, but never in doubt!

My particular brand of schizophrenia has more to do with James' warning: "Wash your hands, you sinners, and purify your hearts, you double-minded." What I firmly and confidently believe as a matter of faith and doctrine doesn't always translate into how I live my life.

If the truth be known, I, the Christian—I, the Christian author and lecturer—am an idolater. Oh, yes, every bit as much as the prophets of Baal. Is not my greed and covetousness idolatry? Do I not attempt to do that which Jesus said was not possible—to simultaneously worship both God and Money?

It doesn't matter that I am by no means the greediest, or the most covetous, or the most materialistic person around. To whatever extent I am greedy, or covetous, or materialistic—or worldly-minded in any other way—I am idolatrous. And to whatever extent I am idolatrous, I am wavering in my allegiance to God.

So I'm glad I drove out of my way to see the Monastery of Muhraqah and its statue of the fierce-looking Elijah. I'm glad I smelled the smoke of the barbecues and the meat cooking on the grill. I'm glad I stopped to eat the forbidden bread with the secular Jews. Because I needed to be reminded.

With the dawning of each new day, I face a crucial contest between two gods. One god seems more real, if only because this world is more immediate and more tangible. Yet the god of this world is powerless when I call out for help. When I am really in need, the world doesn't want to know. There is no response: No one answers, no one pays attention.

The other god, the true and living God, may seem more distant, and therefore less real. But this one thing I know: He has never let me down in my hour of need. Against impossible odds, he has always come through.

Why then do I continue to waver? What sense does it make to split my allegiance between two gods? If only I could borrow Elijah's sword for a day! Then I could whack the "ish" off Christian-*ish*, and be the single-minded *Christian* that God is calling me to be!

If I can learn anything from Elijah's confrontation with the prophets of Baal, surely it is that I must learn to challenge my spiritual enemies, not just coexist with them in an uneasy daily alliance. A failure to confront whatever it is that gets between me and God is simply to capitulate to my enemies, to allow my life to be covered with pagan shrines of all kinds.

Surely, too, Elijah's altar is a reminder that, if I really want to be steadfast in my allegiance to God, then I must be willing to sacrifice some of the things in my life that (so far, at least) I haven't been willing to give up.

But how will I ever be able to give up those things? From what I can see of Elijah's tactics, there is only one way: heartfelt, sincere, fervent prayer—with perhaps an emphasis on fervent. The prophets of Baal weren't wrong to pray in a frenzy. Their problem was that there was no god to hear them. But "praying without ceasing" is a biblical call to prayer. How else but by a "frenzied" commitment to prayer can I hope to build a fire under my desire to sacrifice?

In the end, perhaps the question is not so much whether we are willing to engage in fervent prayer to overcome our persistent vacillation between the things of God and the things of this world. Perhaps the real question is whether we are prepared for God's response. As demonstrated so powerfully in the story of Elijah and the prophets, we're just liable to get what we pray for!

Can you imagine it? A fire coming down out of heaven, consuming every selfish desire, every stubborn will, every wayward thought, every misdirected word, every evil motive? No wonder we drench our altars of prayer in the waters of hesitancy, doubt, and vacillation.

Oh, to have the faith of Elijah! Oh, to have his *courage*!

Lord, your power is too great, too consuming for my
wavering faith. Send me this day the tiniest spark that

might ignite in me a flame of passion for your greater power in my life. Prepare in me a heart willing to accept your overwhelming love, and only then, Lord, pour down upon me the fullness of your Self until my own being is wholly consumed in thine.

Chapter Eighteen

"I am with you

and will rescue you."

JEREMIAH 1:8

Rescue

As walls go, it's not a very pretentious wall. Instead of uniform blocks of dressed granite or other fine stone, this wall is made of nothing more sophisticated than carefully stacked rocks—some huge, some tiny; some holding pride of position, some used as mere filler to hold the larger rocks in place. Compared with the far more elaborate walls in Jerusalem, it definitely has a humble look about it. Even so, it simply has to be one of my favorites.

The wall I'm talking about—the Broad Wall—has none of the pedigree of the other walls, because it was built centuries earlier, in 701 B.C. But, then, that's one of the reasons why I like it so much. Compared to the age of the United States, or civilization in Western Europe, or the Roman Empire, or almost anything else except perhaps the pyramids, it's very, very old. And if for no other reason, very impressive.

Yet the wall's age is only one of the reasons I like it so much. Another reason is that it is one of those ancient structures specifically mentioned in the Old Testament. To see it, all you have to do is enter the Jewish Quarter and find your way to Plugat Hakotel Street. All of a sudden there it is, right before your very eyes: about 150 feet of tangible, live-action biblical history!

Never mind that the wall is not its original height. It is plenty high enough to let you know that, in its original state, it would have been one giant wall. What you get to see for the mere price of half a roll of film is an enormous wall some 23 feet wide—a *broad* wall indeed!

The date reveals not only the wall's age but also its builder—King Hezekiah of Judah, the same Hezekiah of "Hezekiah's Tunnel." The tunnel and the Broad Wall were both constructed at the same time as part of Hezekiah's defenses against King Sennacherib's Assyrian army. The text says that Hezekiah "worked hard repairing all the broken sections of the [original] wall and building towers on it." Then, "he built another wall outside that one," which came to be known even in biblical times as the Broad Wall.

If that were all we knew about the Broad Wall, I would still be excited about seeing it in person. It's ancient. It's biblical. But what really captures my imagination about the wall is being able to catch a true-to-life glimpse of one of my favorite biblical stories.

Oddly, though, it is not the story of Hezekiah, the great king of Judah and architect of monumental building schemes. Rather, it's the story of a relatively unknown Jew in exile named Nehemiah, some three centuries removed. In the course of history it is Nehemiah's name, not Hezekiah's, that has become almost synonymous with the walls of Jerusalem, including the Broad Wall.

I see Nehemiah as one of those heroes we would all like to be: the ordinary guy on the street who gathers his courage in a near-impossible situation and comes flying to the rescue. Not

Superman, but mild-mannered Clark Kent. Not Goliath, but the shepherd boy David. In other words, not some modern-day macho figure, but you and me, getting the job done.

The story of Nehemiah begins with the fall of Judah and the destruction of Jerusalem in 586 B.C. Hezekiah's formidable walls could not withstand either the power of the Babylonian army under Nebuchadnezzar or the judgment of God for Judah's disobedience. So the walls of Jerusalem were broken down and the city was sacked.

It was this defeat, you'll recall, that led to the great exile of the Jews from Israel to Babylonia, which was later succeeded in power by the Persians. King Cyrus was more sympathetic to the Jews than his Babylonian predecessors, and allowed a contingent of the Jews to return and rebuild the temple under the leadership of Zerubbabel and the prophets Haggai and Zechariah. After a number of false starts, the temple was finally completed in 516 B.C., exactly 70 years after it was destroyed—precisely as God had said!

After the passing of some 60 years, a second contingent of the Jews, under the leadership of Ezra, was given permission by Artaxerxes to return to Israel and revitalize the law, which the Persian king greatly admired. But restoration did not come quickly, either politically or spiritually. For another 14 years Israel was beset by enemies from without and a lack of enthusiasm from within. (Ever felt like that yourself? Just kind of spiritually lackadaisical? "On hold" with God?)

It is at this point that the story of Nehemiah picks up. Nehemiah, a Jew in exile, was King Artaxerxes' cupbearer in the Persian capital of Susa. Being a cupbearer was not typical slave duty. It was not unknown in those times for a king to be assassinated by poisoning. The cupbearer, therefore, was more like a Secret Service agent who guarded the life of the king. His was a trusted position. Nevertheless, Nehemiah was not of royal lineage; he had no political power and had no special standing in Persian social circles.

Apart from his highly responsible position, Nehemiah was an ordinary Jew. But there was this about him that was extraordinary: Nehemiah's great faith in the God of the Hebrews had won the respect of King Artaxerxes, a respect which had led to a unique friendship between the king and his Jewish servant. When one day the king noticed that Nehemiah was looking sad and troubled, he inquired about the source of his sadness. It seems that Nehemiah had heard reports that his fellow Jews who had returned to Jerusalem were not faring well at all. There was trouble and disgrace, and the walls of Jerusalem were in shambles.

So what happened? The text tells us matter-of-factly that the king granted Nehemiah's request to go to Jerusalem and oversee the rebuilding of the walls. Excuse me? Nehemiah was going to rebuild the walls of Jerusalem? Pardon my asking, but what special expertise did Nehemiah have to oversee such a task? Who did he, a mere cupbearer, think he was—Hezekiah?

It defies all logic to think that cupbearer Nehemiah could pull off one of the biggest wall-building jobs in history; but if you are familiar with the story, you know the equally incredible ending. The short version is that Nehemiah goes to Jerusalem, surveys the wall by night when no one is looking, sets into place a plan of action, and, within a blistering 52 days, oversees the complete repair of the walls.

For the record, that's *all* of Jerusalem's walls, including the Broad Wall. How did he do it? He took a lesson from Hezekiah's wall itself: Whether large or small, whether impressive or ordinary, each rock had a role to play. Some rocks provided weight, and some provided the strength, but some were merely there to provide unheralded support. Filler rocks, we might call them. Just common, ordinary filler.

What Nehemiah did was to rally the whole community to work together: each in his place, each doing what alone would have been impossible. And here's the part I love: None of the workers had to have prior experience in wall-building to get a job. Willingness was the only requirement.

So we have this fascinating roll call of workers: Eliashib the high priest and his fellow priests rolled up their priestly sleeves and rebuilt the Sheep Gate and the wall adjacent to it, all the way to the Tower of the Hundred. The men of Jericho lent a hand and repaired the adjoining section, from which point Zaccur (whoever he was) built next to them.

And how about these two? Uzziel, a goldsmith, and Hananiah, a perfume-maker, each repaired a section of the walls. Surely not your most likely stonemasons! In fact, it was these two men who, along with all the others, "restored Jerusalem as far as the Broad Wall." There's that wall again! Do you begin to feel the excitement I felt standing above that very same wall?

And what about this timely reference? "Shallum son of Hallohesh, ruler of a half-district of Jerusalem, repaired the next section *with the help of his daughters.*" Names unknown. Faces unseen.

Over and over the text tells us that workers repaired the section of the wall which was "in front of his own house," or "opposite his living quarters," or "beside his house." Just ordinary people repairing the walls nearest them. If some of the workers had come a long way to lend a hand, most were just taking care of whatever needed their attention on the front doorstep. And together they made a job of it, even fighting off their enemies while they worked!

Nothing extraordinary about them. No special expertise. If you passed them on the street, you might be tempted to think of them as "filler." But they weren't just filler; they were heroes! Ordinary people, touched by a great need, coming to the rescue. And within less than two months the walls of Jerusalem had been repaired. Major walls! Giant walls! *Broad* walls!

Do you see why I like the Broad Wall? It takes tiny little filler rocks and makes them important. It takes ordinary people and makes them extraordinary. It takes people like you and me, with common feelings of fear and insecurity and worthlessness, and makes them heroes.

From simple cupbearers God builds mighty walls.

But of course the real story is not about walls at all. You and I are not likely to be called upon to repair a wall of stone to fend off some military enemy. The real story is told by the prophet Isaiah in a passage dealing with, of all things, fasting. What is true fasting, asks Isaiah? And the answer is surprising: "Is not this the kind of fasting I have chosen," says God, "to loose the chains of injustice and untie the cords of the yoke, to set the oppressed free and break every yoke? Is it not to share your food with the hungry and to provide the poor wanderer with shelter—when you see the naked, to clothe him, and not to turn away from your own flesh and blood?"

Just about the time we begin to wonder what possible connection there might be between repairing walls and a sermon on fasting, we hear these call-to-action words from Isaiah: "You will be called Repairer of Broken Walls, Restorer of Streets with Dwellings."

And now it all makes sense: *To do justice is to repair walls; to restore broken lives is to be heroic.*

The story, then, is not at all about rocks and walls, but about *people.* People in need of rescue, and people who come to their rescue. Ordinary people seeing extraordinary needs, and doing whatever it takes to meet those needs.

Want to be a hero? You don't have to wear a cape. Just walk out your front door and look at the human rubble lying everywhere at your feet: the poor, the hungry, the dispossessed, the ignored, the abused. Lift one stone upon another, whether big or small, and before you know it some grateful people whose lives have been turned around will do you great honor.

And then you too shall be called "Repairer of Broken Walls." Together with Nehemiah, you too shall be a wall-builder.

Down in the human heart, crushed by the tempter,
Feelings lie buried that grace can restore;
Touched by a loving hand, wakened by kindness,
Chords that were broken will vibrate once more.

Rescue the perishing, care for the dying;
Jesus is merciful, Jesus will save.

—Fanny J. Crosby

Chapter Nineteen

"Be strong and courageous . . .

for God goes with you."

DEUTERONOMY 31:6

Courage

Not many tour buses head southwest from Jerusalem along the historic road to Gaza. It is the Old City, Jericho, and the Dead Sea that capture the interest of most tourists on the run. Still, a trip down the ancient road to Gaza is an experience not to be missed.

The highway itself is one of the oldest highways still in use today, dating back some 4000 years before Christ. Along the way you can even see some of the old Roman milestone markers. It is along this road that traders and merchants have moved for centuries, and, of course, conquering armies as well. Whether it was Syria, or Babylonia, or Persia, Israel's enemies always approached Jerusalem from the southwest along the Gaza Road.

For the first-time visitor, it is hard to believe how mountainous and forested the Judean countryside is. What a contrast to the rest of Israel! As you drive up and down the steep terrain, you begin to appreciate why the tribes of Judah and Ephraim enjoyed relative peace, compared with the other tribes. The chariots of the Philistines obviously weren't much use high up in these wooded and rocky Judean hills!

As we drove along, we saw several groups of children playing on the hills, enjoying fields of spring flowers in full bloom on a balmy spring day in early April. Red poppies, yellow crown daisies, and purple milk thistles provided a carpet of brilliant color to accent the pristine green of the Judean countryside. And the views were simply spectacular—north to Caesarea, west to the thin blue line of the Mediterranean, and south toward the ancient city of Askelon.

Each stop along the way represented a piece of familiar biblical history. There is, for example, the town of Bet Shemesh, where the Philistines returned the ark of the covenant to Israel by loading it on a cart which was pulled up the Gaza road by two cows. Nearby is the village of Zorah, where Samson was born and raised. Still further south is the city of Gath and the area where Samson frequented the Philistine honky-tonks and met Delilah, the woman who would prove to be his downfall.

In the same region is the now-overrun tel of the ancient Israelite city of Lachish, the ruins of which provide wonderful stories about the Judean kings and those enemies of Israel (like the Assyrian king, Sennacharib) who conquered the fortress and made it their own headquarters as they mounted attacks against Jerusalem.

But, for me, one stop along the Gaza Road made my whole day. Right there beside the road was a washed-out gully—dry, but clearly the bed of a creek which in another season might have been filled with water. Overlooking the dry creek bed on either side were two hills, forming between them a kind of amphitheater, as if the perfect setting for a great drama. And indeed a great drama had been played out at that very spot—a drama almost unparalleled for sheer suspense and excitement. In fact, it has to be among my earliest childhood memories, told both in stories and in song: the great confrontation between David and Goliath.

The story surely needs no retelling. Standing there in the middle of that natural amphitheater, it was easy to imagine the well-trained, well-fed Philistine army facing down the scraggly band of Israelite warriors who had come west from Hebron to meet their formidable enemies. In fact, that is why David was there in the first place. The Israelites were so poorly maintained that the soldiers' families had to send food to the front lines. David had come to the Valley of Elah only because his father, Jesse, had commissioned David to carry food to his three brothers who were serving in Saul's ragtag army.

When David arrives, he learns of the Philistines' offer to resolve the conflict through a one-on-one fight between two champions of the respective sides. Under normal circumstances, it might have sounded like a good idea, but the Philistines' champion was a nine-foot-tall giant named Goliath who, quite understandably, terrified Saul and his men.

But David sized up the situation and sensed a unique opportunity to honor the Lord's name. Besides that, rumor had it that the king would handsomely reward any man among his army who killed Goliath, not only with money and a tax-free status for the man's family, but also by giving the king's daughter in marriage. Defending God's honor and getting a wife in the process—what more could a young man ask?

Like David's own brothers, King Saul thought David's offer to fight Goliath was crazy. But David insisted that he was up to the task, citing his experience at having killed both a lion and a bear. Having no better offer, Saul reluctantly agreed to the greatest mismatch in all of history. David even refused to wear the king's armor, saying he wasn't used to its weight and awkwardness.

The conclusion of the story is what made David a legend in his own time. David went down to the stream, chose five small stones, and confidently stepped up to challenge Goliath. As Goliath taunted David and the Israelites, David put one of the stones into his sling and sent it flying straight to Goliath's forehead. Goliath fell to the ground, and David cut off his head with Goliath's own sword. At that the Philistines fled and the Israelites won the day.

From that moment forward, David was known far and wide for his courage. Call him opportunistic and foolhardy if you wish, but there can be no doubting his courage, a courage based in large measure upon a deep-seated faith in the power of the God of Israel.

The saga of David and Goliath is high drama, especially for young minds which delight in underdog heroes beating up on nasty villains. Even for those of us who are older, it is a fantasy fulfilled. Have you never dreamed about saving some helpless child from a high-rise fire? Or about taking over the controls from the dying pilot of a jumbo jet and saving its 300 passengers? There is something in all of us that wants to be a hero—which, if I'm right about it, translates pretty directly into a deep desire to be courageous. Probably more courageous than we know we could ever be in real life.

As I thought about David's courage, I climbed down into the dry creek bed and looked up at its steep banks. Not even Goliath could have seen David as he reached down and chose those five smooth stones. What must it have been like for David down there? Did his courage preclude all fear? Surely not. Did his confidence in God mean he wasn't the least bit apprehensive? I doubt it.

What *is* important is not that David felt true fear and apprehension—as any of us would—but that he acted courageously in spite of that fear. *Acting in the face of fear*, not *fearlessness*, is true courage. True courage is overcoming the fear that is natural to a given situation. It is the courage of Jesus, who in the face of certain death asked, "If at all possible, let this cup pass from me," yet unwaveringly submitted to the inevitable.

Before leaving the creek bed, I reached down as David had done centuries ago and carefully chose five small stones. Not too large, not too small. They had to be just right. What I needed was a handful of courage to carry away with me.

After all, there is a battle going on out there. All around me I see Goliaths taunting me and threatening to cause me harm. But, just as David had told Goliath, he would also remind us today, that "it is not by sword or spear that the LORD saves; for the battle is the LORD's and he will give all of you into our hands." Of course, that was easy for *David* to say. Hadn't God given the lion and the bear into David's hand? Why shouldn't David be courageous?

Then again, hasn't God given *us* victories in the past, even against great odds? Hasn't he demonstrated his love and protection over us each day that we live? So why should we think that he would abandon us in our greatest hour of need? In the lessons of the past we can take courage for the future.

As I mulled over that thought, I climbed up out of the creek bed and back onto the Gaza Road running beside it. And then it struck me: Somewhere along this same road had been another, quite different, act of courage. No, not a heroic act in the heat of some military battle, nor an act which anyone would consider particularly brave. But it was certainly a great act of *spiritual* courage.

If the road to Gaza is known for anything, it is the conversion of the Ethiopian eunuch. For it was down this very road that the

Ethiopian queen's treasury official was traveling in a chariot when an angel of the Lord said to the evangelist, Philip, "Go south to the road—the desert road—that goes down from Jerusalem to Gaza." As Philip ran up to the chariot, the eunuch asked Philip's help in understanding a passage which he was reading from the prophet Isaiah. Drawing from that passage, Philip began to proclaim to him the good news of Jesus, the Messiah of whom Isaiah had prophesied.

Convinced that Jesus was indeed his Savior and Lord, the eunuch noticed some water alongside the road and said to Philip: "Look, here is water. Why shouldn't I be baptized?" So the chariot was stopped, and Philip baptized the eunuch immediately at that very place.

What place? What water? Was it a pool or a stream? If it was a stream, could it possibly have been the same stream where David picked up the five stones?

I knew the moment I asked myself those questions that the odds of such a geographical coincidence were remote indeed. But I confess that I *wanted* it to be true, because there is a very real sense in which the Ethiopian eunuch was every bit as courageous as David.

Putting one's life into the hands of the Lord is always a courageous act, whether it be in the heat of conflict or at the point of one's personal faith commitment. In either instance we join with Jesus in his own last act of courage, saying, "Father, into your hands I commit my spirit."

Could there possibly be a more defining moment in any of our lives? Could anything be more daunting than putting our complete trust in God, and God alone?

Rolling around five little stones in my hand, I hesitated for a moment more on the Gaza Road, took renewed courage, and then, like the Ethiopian eunuch, went on my way rejoicing!

Chapter Twenty

"I will perpetuate

your memory

through all generations."

PSALM 45:17

Storytelling

At precisely 6:24 P.M. the ram's horn was blown and the candles were lit. It was Passover in Jerusalem. Fittingly for a pilgrim feast, the guests for the seder meal were from all over the globe: Germany, Holland, Latvia, Kenya, Finland, Ukraine, South Africa, Korea, the United States, and, of course, Israel. Our very presence seemed to confirm the words which would be spoken during the seder: "Next year in Jerusalem!" For us, "next year" had come.

But this was not to be a typical seder meal. This particular group of Jews who had gathered to celebrate the Passover (or "Pesach" in Hebrew) were not simply Jews, but Messianic Jews. If, for Jews, Pesach is a celebration of the coming out of Egypt, for Messianic Jews it is also a celebration of the coming of the Pascal Lamb—Jesus the Messiah! For these believers, Pesach was a "double remembrance," not only of deliverance from slavery, but of deliverance from sin. Hence the seder meal on the first night of the Passover would be observed with all the ritual and tradition with which it has been imbued over the centuries, yet celebrated in light of the good news of the Messiah's appearance.

And what a meal it was! Not so much the food, but the ceremony, which combined all the best elements of a worship service, a party, a classroom lesson, and a holiday homecoming. In prayer-book fashion we followed the words in the Haggada, which led us through the various recitations, prayers, songs, and rituals for the evening.

The centerpiece of the seder was the matza, or unleavened bread—the same bread eaten by the children of Israel on their flight from Egypt. So at various times we broke the matza, hid the matza, and ate the matza. We also drank, not just one or two, but four cups of either wine or grape juice. For Christians, the parallels with the bread and wine of the Lord's Supper were unmistakable: Christ's body; Christ's blood.

There were also the bitter herbs (parsley or celery leaves dipped in saltwater)—a reminder of the suffering of Jews. "For, not one persecutor only has risen to destroy us; but in every generation there are those who rise to destroy us." And there was also the "sandwich" made of matza and a sweet compote of apples, dates, bananas, raisins, almonds, walnuts, and cinnamon. "There is always both bitter and sweet. God never gives a harsh judgment without a message of consolation."

For those of us who are spiritual sons and daughters of Abraham, the Messiah's *bitter crucifixion* is our *sweet salvation*. The symbolic egg may have been my personal favorite. "The Jews are like a boiled egg," Joseph, our host, told us through a wry smile, worn as a badge of pride. "The longer you boil them, the harder they get!"

The actual meal itself, including matza-ball soup, lamb, potatoes, carrots, and salad, was—for my tastes—somewhat anti-climactic. Or maybe I was just remembering my small part in its preparation: rinsing the salt out of the lamb after it had been rubbed in to help remove the blood from the flesh. It wasn't a pretty sight! But the final product was tasty enough, and filling.

Throughout the Passover seder, the focus was always on the children. Indeed, they were the object of the whole exercise, and have been from the very first Passover. Remember what Moses told the Israelites? "When you enter the land that the LORD will give you as he promised, observe this ceremony. And when your children ask you, 'What does this ceremony mean to you?' then tell them, 'It is the Passover sacrifice to the LORD, who passed over the houses of the Israelites in Egypt and spared our homes when he struck down the Egyptians.'"

Traditionally, then, the youngest child at the seder asks "The Four Questions":

On all other nights we may eat either Hamez or
Matza; why on this night only Matza?

On all other nights we eat other kinds of herbs:
why on this night bitter herbs?

On all other nights we do not even dip the herbs
once; why on this night do we dip twice?

On all other nights we eat either sitting or
reclining; why on this night do we all recline?

The remainder of the Haggada is essentially the answer to those questions, centering on the story of the Exodus, which has symbolized the history of the Jews ever since then. For Jewish children, especially, the Haggada is a retelling of the story, a transmission of tradition, and an indoctrination into the Jewish soul. From start to finish, the Haggada is aimed at achieving one result: "In every single generation, it is a man's duty to think of himself as one of those who came out of Egypt."

If it was an important message, it was also a marathon message, lasting some four hours. By the end of the evening I detected more than one nodding head among the older adults. So just imagine the restlessness of the younger children. Given their typically short attention spans, one senses that there was method in the madness of hiding a piece of the matza at the beginning of the seder. When the seder is concluded, the child who finds the missing matza is rewarded by being given whatever he or she asks. (Within reason, of course!) For most of the children, then, the thought of such a generous reward is more than adequate incentive to stay awake and stay tuned.

As a further reward for all the children, there were a number of songs which were sung just for their benefit. One song, entitled "Who Knows One?", was reminiscent of "The Twelve Days of Christmas," with its repetitive add-on lyrics. (God is one. The tablets of the covenant are two. The patriarchs—Abraham, Isaac, and Jacob—are three. And so forth, down to the 13 attributes of God.)

That song reminded me of the many little children's songs I was taught in Sunday school and, even more so, during the week of vacation Bible school each summer. The songs were both fun and action-filled! Energetically acting out the words, we marched in the Lord's army, hurled stones at Goliath, rocked the baby Jesus, and clapped when the foolish man's house fell flat! Before we could even memorize book, chapter, and verse, we were thoroughly familiar with the stories of the Bible.

I love that part of my heritage. I love *sharing* that part of my heritage. Isn't that what another little camp song encourages us to do: "Pass it on"?

What's made to be fun for the children turns out to be not just storytelling but serious theology at a level that children can understand: There is one God. There were two tablets of the covenant. There were three patriarchs, four matriarchs, five books of the Torah, and so on. When it comes to learning, children are never too young. Nor are they ever more inquisitive.

Like Moses before him, Joshua counted on the natural curiosity of little children to perpetuate the story of Israel's miraculous history. When the Israelites crossed into the Promised Land, Joshua instructed the men of Israel to take 12 stones from the middle of the Jordan River and to erect them as a memorial of their crossing. "In the future, when your children ask you, 'What do these stones mean?' tell them that the flow of the Jordan was cut off before the ark of the covenant of the LORD."

Whether stacks of stones, or Passover seders, or the ultimate meaning of life, each succeeding generation must ask all of the same questions for itself. If the two-year-old's incessant *"Why?"* can drive a person to distraction, nevertheless it is God's way of keeping his message alive from generation to generation. With all the insistence that a two-year-old can muster, the demand is universal and timeless: "Tell me the story! What is the mystery of life?"

As the Pesach celebration reminds us, the questioning process presupposes that the child is observing something which prompts the question. For Jewish children, it may be questions about the seder meal; or, in centuries past, about a pile of 12 stones by the Jordan River.

In our own context, we must be doing something right when a child's mind intuitively asks: "Why is one day of the week different from all the others?" Or at church, "Why are they passing around the bread and wine?" and "Why is that person being dunked in the water?" On the home front, perhaps it's "Why do my parents keep reading that one particular book every day?" or "Why do we always pray at bedtime?"

As any parent knows, these simple acts never go unnoticed by children. It's how they learn, how they ultimately live, and what they themselves will eventually bequeath to their own children, "even to children yet to be born."

The incredible prospect of that far-extended future intrigues me no end. Generations from now, what will they believe? How will they live? And, of immediate importance, what influence am I having right now over people I will never know in decades and centuries to come? "A good man," says the proverb, "leaves an inheritance for his children's children."

It's a sobering thought, isn't it? What inheritance am I leaving for generations yet unborn?

Today I reread some familiar words from the pen of the prophet Joel, writing more than 28 centuries ago: "Tell it to your children, and let your children tell it to their children, and their children to the next generation." What an irony, I thought. Joel could never have guessed that, all these centuries later, I would be listening to what he had to say, and still be prompted by it.

It simply proves the point: Neither the story nor its telling ever ends. Unless, of course, I myself stop the telling.

So when the little ones in my life beg to be read "just one more story," may God give me the patience to read it. May God also give me the wisdom to know that they are listening attentively to every other "story" I share in their presence, whether I have an open book before me or not.

In the eyes of precious little ones, every moment is a story; every life, a seder.

Chapter Twenty-one

"Submit to God

and be at peace

with him."

JOB 22:21

Submission

What strikes you most about the Garden of Gethsemane is its peacefulness. (At least, after all the tour buses have left for the day.) It's a place in which you want to sit down. To reflect. To pray. No wonder Jesus often came to Gethsemane to get away from all the pressure. No wonder he came there to pray.

It is also one of the few places where you can personally experience something almost exactly the way Jesus himself would have experienced it. Although it's possible that the Romans destroyed the original olive trees in the garden when they sacked Jerusalem, it is also possible that they didn't. And if they didn't, some of the very trees that stand there today may well have stood vigil over Jesus as he prayed.

What also impresses the first-time visitor is how close Gethsemane is to the eastern wall of Jerusalem. At most, it's a ten-minute walk from the Golden Gate, down through the narrow Kidron Valley, and back up to the base of the western slope of the Mount of Olives. Although the Golden Gate is now blocked up, it would have been the gate through which the soldiers would have come to arrest Jesus in the garden.

Resting beneath one of the gnarly olive trees, I tried to imagine what it would be like in the dark of night as Jesus turned and saw the procession slowly making its way out through the Golden Gate and across the Kidron. He would easily have seen the torches and lanterns being carried by the soldiers and the officials from the chief priests. Surely his apprehension must have increased with every step they took toward him.

But go back slightly, to the point where Jesus and his disciples leave the upper room and go out to the Mount of Olives. As they enter the Garden of Gethsemane, Jesus leaves most of the disciples near the entrance and invites Peter, James, and John to go with him a bit further into the garden. Jesus is beginning to feel deeply the agony of the ordeal he is about to face. "My soul is overwhelmed with sorrow to the point of death," he tells them. "Stay here and keep watch with me."

Going a stone's throw beyond the three disciples, Jesus prays alone, his face to the ground. Perhaps even more than the much-recited "Lord's Prayer," the words that he prays in the garden have become immortalized both for their poignancy and their power.

First comes the prayer of every person who has ever faced the excruciating pain of suffering or the fearful prospect of immediate death: "My Father, if it is possible, may this cup be taken from me." Then comes the prayer that so many of us wish we could pray, but find so difficult to utter: "Yet not as I will, but as you will."

After an hour in agonizing prayer, Jesus returns to the three disciples and finds them sleeping. Seemingly out of character, Jesus rebukes them for falling asleep. "Could you men not keep watch with me for one hour?" he asks Peter brusquely.

It's late, and the disciples are tired. Unlike Jesus, they don't have a clue what is about to happen (although they should, for he had clearly told them). Then Jesus says, "Watch and pray so that you will not fall into temptation. The spirit is willing, but the body is weak."

Leaving them startled and somewhat bewildered, Jesus goes away for a second time and repeats his earlier prayer. Then he returns, only to find that the three have gone back to sleep. This time he does not disturb them, but leaves again to pray for a third time. By now his anguish is so great that his sweat is like "drops of blood falling to the ground."

Yet how can that be? At the thought of the Son of God sweating in agony, all I know about the trinity, or about the incarnation, or "the Word made flesh" evaporates into the evening mist of the garden. Did not the Son of God already know the outcome? Surely so. But he was also the Son of Man. Like you and me, Jesus was fully human. So for even the Son of God, the cross would be no harmless charade. His suffering would not be a circus sideshow. When Jesus prayed in torment to his "Abba Father" in Gethsemane, he was engaged in a genuine life-and-death struggle.

Because I know all too well what it is like to struggle between my spirit (which is eagerly willing) and my human nature (which is frustratingly weak), I want to know more about Jesus' prayers that night. In the dramatic brevity of the events which are recorded for us in the Gospels, we are given only an encapsulated sound bite: If possible, give me a way of escape; if not, I'll do whatever must be done.

But surely there had to be more. In the case of the first prayer alone, there had to be *a full hour more*. What else did Jesus say to his Father? What can I say to mine when I find myself in Jesus' shoes?

It's just a hunch, of course—indeed, pure speculation. But for all the times Jesus had come to Gethsemane to be alone and pray, surely it must have occurred to him that someone from his own lineage had prayed there centuries before, perhaps in that very same spot. King David himself had stopped on the Mount of Olives to pray as he was fleeing from his son Absalom. And, on this night of nights, in the depths of his own agony, surely it would not have escaped Jesus that David's prayer, too, was said in a time of deepest sorrow and in anticipation of unthinkable betrayal.

I wonder, then, if Jesus might not have lifted up David's prayer once again to God. Every line of it is filled with symbolism for Jesus' own moment of suffering:

> *O LORD, how many are my foes!*
> *How many rise up against me!*
> *Many are saying of me,*
> *"God will not deliver him."*

> *But you are a shield around me, O LORD;*
> *you bestow glory on me and lift up my head.*
> *To the LORD I cry aloud,*
> *and he answers me from his holy hill.*

> *I lie down and sleep;*
> *I wake again, because the LORD sustains me.*

I will not fear the tens of thousands
drawn up against me on every side.

Arise, O LORD!
Deliver me, O my God!
Strike all my enemies on the jaw;
break the teeth of the wicked.

From the LORD comes deliverance.
May your blessing be on your people.

I shiver just thinking about how incredibly apropos each word of David's prayer would have been for Jesus that night: "Foes." "Holy hill." "Sleep." "Deliverance."

Jesus was not just the Son of God or the Son of Man. He was also the Son of David. The interwoven threads of the scriptural tapestry never cease to amaze me. Here were two kings, centuries apart, related by blood, related by circumstance, related by the human struggle which binds us all.

I also can't help but think that Jesus must have appreciated the grand irony which further linked his own personal struggle with that of David's. The prayer of David had been occasioned by a rebellious, disobedient son who was betraying his own father. Jesus' prayer, by contrast, reflected the heart of an obedient son— a son who, though tempted to disobey, was determined to honor his father.

Isn't that what he had been taught from boyhood to do? Did not the law mandate death by stoning for a rebellious son? Yet what an impossible dilemma! If Jesus submitted to the will of his Father, he would die a cruel death on the cross. If he refused to submit, he would still be worthy of death by stoning under the law!

Of course, Jesus knew, as well as you and I know, that if he fled into some comfortable exile, no one was going to stone him to death for disobeying "his Father." Faced, on the other hand, with the immediate, inevitable reality of a tortuous death if he actually chose to submit, the stakes were at a premium. Disobedience meant potential freedom; obedience meant certain death.

Confronted with such a choice, Jesus had come to the right spot. (Gethsemane means "olive press.") With his face pressed to the ground in agony, the Son of Man was feeling, like never before, the pressure he had come here so often to escape. For now, not only his fate, but the fate of the world was hanging in the balance. *Your* fate and *mine*.

And when Jesus was pressed until there was nothing left to squeeze, what oozed out of him was not just sweat like drops of blood, but submission. Humble, obedient submission.

"And he was heard because of his reverent submission. Although he was a son, he learned obedience from what he suffered and, once made perfect, he became the source of eternal salvation for all who obey him . . . ."

So now it's my turn to experience Gethsemane. Not just the calming moments of peace in the shade of an ancient olive tree, nor warm-fuzzy reflections back centuries to a time when Jesus himself prayed in this very garden, but the painful prospect of total commitment. Will I surrender my life completely in obedience to him who surrendered his own life for me, or will I follow in the rebellious footsteps of Absalom?

I don't know about you, but for me, submission is not easy. I don't like having to obey. I'm a wild stallion that doesn't want to be tamed. I'm a two-year-old whose favorite words are "Mine!" and "No!" I'm a lawyer always looking for a loophole. *"Father, if it is at all possible, take this cup from me!"*

Reflecting at length on my own stubborn self-will eventually lulls me into a prolonged stupor. Then, as if transported back through time, I wake from my reverie and hear Jesus saying to me, "Could you not keep watch with me for one hour?" And, when I see the tears in his eyes, I know that he is asking of me no more than what he had to ask of himself.

Just then we hear the voices of the soldiers and see their torches as they come into the garden to surround us. I look at Jesus and see the face of One who, having struggled mightily with his own human vulnerability, has boldly determined to do the right thing. One glance from Jesus, and I know he is asking, "What about you? What are you going to do?"

I look down, to nothing in particular. I look up, wanting desperately to say, *"Your will, not mine."* But I can't begin to utter it. My lips tremble, and almost move, but there is no sound.

Suddenly there is a comforting hand on my shoulder and a knowing look from the suffering Son of Man. "O my son Absalom!" he says to me. "My son, my son Absalom! If only I had died instead of you—O Absalom, my son, my son!"

And before I know what has happened, he is gone out of the garden . . . to do just that.

> *When my love to Christ grows weak,*
> *When for deeper faith I seek,*
> *Then in thought I go to Thee,*
> *Garden of Gethsemane!*

There I walk amid the shades,
While the ling'ring twilight fades,
See that suffering, friendless One,
Weeping, praying there alone.

Then to life I turn again,
Learning all the worth of pain,
Learning all the might that lies,
In a full self-sacrifice.

—John R. Wreford

Chapter Twenty-two

"There is hope

for your future."

Jeremiah 31:17

Future

It was sheer serendipity. Or was it providence?

We had been told that, because of the political unrest, we should not attempt to walk from the Old City up to the Mount of Olives and on to Bethany. Palestinians in the area were known to harass any strangers invading their space. But having already been to the Garden of Gethsemane, at the foot of the Mount of Olives, I was determined to go all the way to Bethany—whatever the risk.

Should I strike out on my own and just take a chance? Should I settle for second-best and take an Arab taxi as a friendly escort? As I thought about the options one evening while sitting in the reading room of the YMCA hotel, I couldn't quite make up my mind.

Just then I looked up and was surprised to see Moses, our breakfast waiter, walking through the lobby. I say "surprised," because it was 9:30 at night and I knew that Moses started work each morning by at least 7:00 A.M. "Had he worked a 14-hour shift today?" I wondered.

I called out to him and, with a quizzical face, pointed to my watch as if to say, "What are you doing here so late?" Moses' weary eyes lit up with recognition and we moved to greet each other. Sure enough, Moses had had a long day. Just like every day.

"No holidays," he said tersely. "I work every day."

Spurred on by a growing friendship developed during our brief breakfast conversations over the prior two weeks, I was curious to know more about Moses' life and circumstances.

"How many children do you have?" I asked.

"Seven," he replied, half-smiling, half-chagrined. "I *must* work!"

At that we had a good laugh. Then came the bonanza question of the day: "Where do you live?"

His surprising response, "On the Mount of Olives," seemed an answer to prayer.

"Mount of Olives?" I blurted out. "Really?" Here at last was a way to solve my dilemma. Who better than Moses would know whether there was any risk to my planned enterprise? "Is it safe to walk to Bethany?" I asked eagerly.

Moses gave me one of those "Are you crazy?" looks and said, "Of course. Who says not?" Weakly protesting that many people had warned me, I could tell that Moses was, to say the least, defensive. Such a suggestion was an insult to his community, and, in an indirect way, to him personally.

"You come to my house for coffee," he said sternly. This was not just an invitation; it was a command! So it was settled. On Saturday Moses would work only half a day, and Ruth and I would meet him after work.

As we ascended the Mount of Olives, we stopped just briefly beneath the luxurious Seven Arches Hotel and took pictures of the Old City across the Kidron Valley. It was a spectacular view, marred only by the two photo session camels waiting on the sidewalk for more enthusiastic tourists than ourselves, and by a pushy hawker brashly trying to sell us scenes of Jerusalem. When we showed no interest in what the man was selling, his once-friendly banter quickly turned to insults. Moses seemed to be particularly irritated by his fellow Arab's rudeness, as if the very myth he was trying to dispel was being perpetuated instead.

So we went quickly on to Moses' house, which turned out to be a surprisingly nice, almost-new home with a fabulous panoramic view over Bethany, from the green hills south toward Bethlehem to the brown hills east toward the Dead Sea. As we came into the yard, we were greeted by the happy faces of Moses' young children, curious about the guests they had been eagerly expecting. I was sure that Westerners, especially Americans, were not usual company for these politically quarantined Arab children.

After briefly greeting us, Moses' smiling wife, Zinab, headed for the kitchen to make, not just the coffee we had been invited for, but what turned out to be a sumptuous lunch of grilled chicken, ground beef patties topped with stewed tomatoes, broiled potatoes stuffed with spicy beef, two different salads, pita bread, olives, and an assortment of dips and relishes. Finally came the Turkish coffee, which, with a little sugar, Ruth said was tolerable enough for Western tastes. I settled for mint tea, which was delicious.

We were surprised when Moses seemed open to discussing religion. On the way up to his house I had asked if he were a Muslim, and he had said yes. Relaxing after a good meal, Moses seemed quite at ease asking us about our own faith.

"Are you Catholic? Protestant?"

He seemed intrigued when I said, "No, we are neither one. We are just Christians, like the first ones."

At that he began to explain as best he could with his elementary English how his Muslim faith differed from Christianity. Of seemingly particular concern to him was the Christian belief that Jesus was the Son of God.

"How could God have son?" he demanded over and over. "God never marry. Not have wife."

As you can appreciate, it is difficult enough under normal circumstances to explain how God, who is spirit, can have a flesh-and-blood son. But explaining the trinity and the incarnation to someone who has difficulty understanding English, and whose only knowledge of the Gospels is what he has heard at the local mosque, is an almost insurmountable task!

From his perspective, if God's having a son wasn't close to being blasphemous (suggesting that God must have been sexually involved with a woman), at the very least it meant that there was more than the one God of Islam—and that surely wouldn't do!

Our gracious host was willing to concede that Jesus was one of many prophets (including Muhammad) who were sent by God to teach us how to be good people. But Moses insisted over and over that Jesus did not die, and that he definitely was not resurrected from any grave. What happened, Moses explained, was that God took Jesus up into heaven, and that, at the end of time, Jesus will return to earth and live for 40 years before the great day of judgment.

With that we were at least making progress! But if you're hoping for a conversion ending to this story, I'm afraid I'll have to disappoint you. At least for now. . . .

What so intrigued me about our conversation with Moses was that it was taking place almost exactly where Jesus did in fact ascend into heaven after his death and resurrection. If, some 20 centuries later, there is still debate and controversy over who Jesus was, I cannot help but think that there is an even greater mystery which I, for one, rarely contemplate: the nature of Jesus' ascension.

Most of us who are believers are quite comfortable discussing Jesus' death, burial, and resurrection. But how often do we contemplate Jesus' ascension? How many hymns are written about what seems to be little more than an epilogue to Jesus' ministry? How many sermons preached?

Perhaps we're thrown off by the relatively little scriptural ink devoted to the event. The ever-so-brief biblical accounts tell us only that Jesus led his disciples up the Mount of Olives to the vicinity of Bethany, lifted his hands, and blessed them. Then "he was taken up before their very eyes, and a cloud hid him from their sight."

That's all there is. No trumpets; no fanfare; not even the horses and chariots of fire which appeared when the prophet Elijah was taken up into heaven. On earth one moment; in heaven the next.

However, Luke does give us a fascinating footnote. As the disciples were looking up into the sky, suddenly two men dressed in white appeared. They said, "Why do you stand here looking into the sky? This same Jesus, who has been taken from you into heaven, will come back in the same way you have seen him go into heaven."

Wow! Even though I missed Jesus' ascension, I could easily be an eyewitness to his return. What an incredible thought!

Little wonder so many believers today are seemingly consumed with predicting the time of Jesus' second coming. Who could blame them, except for Jesus' own admonition that "no one knows about that day or hour, not even the angels in heaven, nor the Son, but only the Father." Yet the promise of his coming remains. Wouldn't it be grand if our generation were privileged to be alive at Jesus' return?

But do I detect a note of caution in the question of the two angels: "Why do you stand here looking into the sky?" What I think I hear them saying to me is, "Don't fix your attention solely on Jesus' reappearance. Keep your eyes on the mission he has left you on earth to accomplish."

Otherwise we might be setting ourselves up for needless disappointment. As much as my father and grandmother, and her father, and his father too, looked forward expectantly to Jesus' coming again, they were never privileged to see it happen. Perhaps my forbears would disapprove, but I think I know when the world will end. I'm virtually certain it will be within the next 25 to 50 years. You see, in another few short years, I won't be living any longer—and that means *my world* will have ended!

Isn't that what really matters? In contrast to all the speculation about the end of time, and despite the glut of popular prophetic predictions, there is nothing speculative about how much more time *I* have on this earth. In human terms, maybe a few decades. Maybe a year. Maybe tomorrow. On the scale of eternity, my departure is but a fleeting breath away.

And then what? For me, that's the burning question: not What will it be like when the Lord returns, but What will it be like when my own soul slips the bonds of this mortal coil and wings its way to God?

If the prospect of Christ's second coming seems exciting and joyous, the prospect of my own "first going" is fraught with apprehension and uncertainty. Despite my hope in Christ, I'm as fearful of the unknown as the next person. If heaven invites, death seems hostile.

But then, so did the Mount of Olives until a friend took me there. And now I think I've been given a wonderful parable. Like my friend Moses, Jesus heard that I had misgivings about my journey into his realm. So today he insisted that I come to the Mount of Olives, to his own place of ascension, and there he showed me, not just future hope, but present peace.

I was expecting a cup of coffee. I came away having shared a spiritual feast.

Chapter Twenty-three

"Lead us not

into temptation."

Matthew 6:13

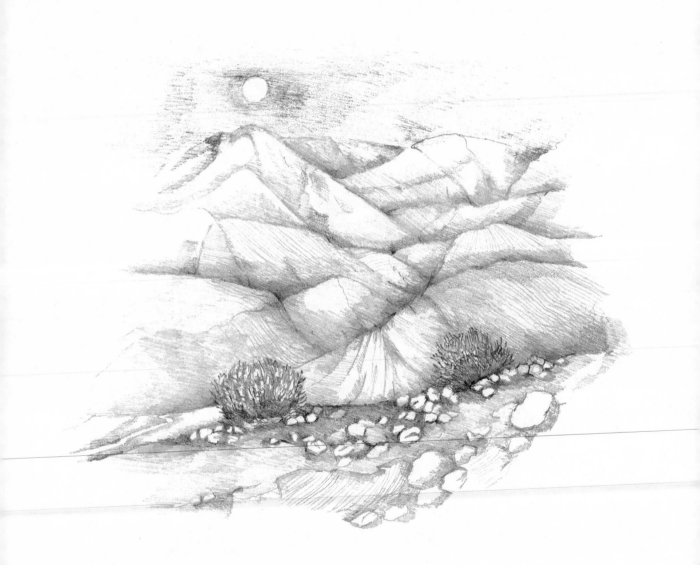

Temptation

Remote. Barren. Foreboding. The Judean Desert is not a place anyone would want to get lost in. Or hungry. Or thirsty. Every time I look to the west from Jericho and see the flat-topped Mountain of Temptation, as it is called, I shake my head in disbelief. It was somewhere out there in that desolate waste-land that Jesus spent 40 days alone, fasting and praying as he began his ministry.

This area of the Judean Desert is known in Arabic as *Qarantal*, or "forty," with reference to the number of days Jesus fasted. That word always reminds me of the Israelites, whose own wandering in the desert lasted 40 years. And when they were hungry, God sent them manna from heaven to sustain them. If Jesus was to be our "manna from heaven," did he somehow need to experience what it is like to be hungry?

Here in the desert, Jesus was confronted by his arch-adversary, the devil. Just as the devil had first appeared in the Garden to test whether man could become God, the devil was more than curious about whether God could become man. Could "the

Word-made-flesh" be tempted to eat when he was hungry? Could the incarnate God resist the opportunity to show off? Could the King of kings refuse having easy sway over the nations of the world?

As he always does, the devil chose just the perfect moment to, if possible, derail Jesus' ministry. He waited until Jesus had just had a "mountaintop experience"—his baptism in the Jordan. The voice from heaven had said, "This is my Son, whom I love; with him I am well pleased." Could there possibly be a headier experience, or one more likely to produce the kind of pride that goes before a fall?

And, of course, Jesus had to be hungry after 40 days of fasting. And undoubtedly weak. (If I fast for a day, I consider it a triumph. Can you imagine what it would be like not to eat for well over a month?) So it is at this point of human weakness that the devil makes his first strike.

"If you are the Son of God," says the tempter, "tell these stones to become bread." But Jesus (who would later multiply the loaves and fish for others who were hungry) will not be goaded. "It is written," says Jesus to his cunning adversary, "'Man does not live on bread alone, but on every word that comes from the mouth of God.'"

Then the scene shifts from the desert to Jerusalem and the pinnacle of the temple. The devil offers Jesus the chance to show what he's made of—to jump off the temple and let everyone watch as legions of angels swoop down to save him just in the nick of time! That would certainly be good theater! But once again Jesus declines the show, reminding the devil that "it is also written: 'Do not put the LORD your God to the test.'"

I suspect that what Satan really wanted to learn from these encounters with Jesus was how much trouble he could count on during Jesus' ministry. Just exactly what will Jesus' game plan be while he's on the earth?

Bravely concealing his own nervous apprehension about Jesus' purpose and power, the devil offers Jesus one last chance to demonstrate any real threat he might pose to the tempter's usurped "authority" on earth.

The devil takes Jesus to a high mountain—quite possibly the "Mountain of Temptation," from which Jesus could have seen four major kingdoms in the region: Moab, Edom, Syria, and Israel. He then has the audacity to offer Jesus all the kingdoms of the world, if only Jesus will bow down and worship him!

At that suggestion, Jesus rightly becomes angry. The devil knows as well as Jesus that it is written: "Worship the Lord your God, and serve him only."

Strangely reassured in his own mind that Jesus was not going to play hardball or throw his weight around while on the earth, the devil smugly took his leave. Little did he know that it was Jesus who had triumphed in that first head-to-head competition. The bully always thinks he has won, but the true champion is the one who is smart enough to walk away and let the bully think what he may. Jesus knew that the real battle had not yet begun!

The writer of Hebrews assures us that "we do not have a high priest who is unable to sympathize with our weaknesses, but we have one who has been tempted in every way, just as we are—yet was without sin." But in what ways, "just as we are," was Jesus tempted, and how did he deal with the kinds of temptations which we face each day?

What did he do, for example, when a "little white lie" might simply have saved him—or perhaps someone else—a lot of grief? Did he even *think* about fudging on the truth? And how did he handle his natural male hormones when some devastatingly beautiful woman passed by? Where did he draw the line between appreciation and lust?

And I'd just about give my proverbial right arm to know precisely what it means to be angry without sinning! Here was a man who had sharp words for his enemies, and even sometimes for his own disciples. Here was a man who took a whip and drove the moneychangers from the temple. Yet we describe his kind of outrage as "righteous indignation." Is that the same kind of "righteous indignation" I have when some driver cuts me off on the highway? Somehow I don't think so. So how did Jesus do it? How did he approach the line of sinful anger without crossing over it?

In my own life, oddly enough, one of my greatest temptations is to shirk moral responsibility altogether—to run away and hide from temptation. To escape into some "desert" where Satan could never find me. And of course I'm not alone in that thought. Isn't that one of the more compelling reasons for the many monasteries that have been established over the centuries—to be separated from the world's enticements, to be cocooned in purity?

There are several such monasteries in the Judean Desert, including one on the Mountain of Temptation. Yet apparently not even the monastery was sufficient isolation for one particular monk. He lived alone in a nearby cave for over 50 years, nourished only by a daily bucket of food and water lowered to him by the other monks!

Yet for Jesus the desert was not a place to *hide* from temptation but to *confront* it head-on! Instead of hiding away, it should be enough simply to know three things that God has promised about temptation: That "no temptation has seized you except what is common to man"; that "God is faithful [and] will not let you be tempted beyond what you can bear"; and that "when you are tempted, he will also provide a way out so that you can stand up under it."

Of course, we should not expect that God is going to haul us out of trouble every time we go racing headlong toward it. By then it's too late. By then we've already gone through the process of temptation which James describes so vividly: "Each one is tempted when, by his own evil desire, he is dragged away and enticed. Then, after desire has conceived, it gives birth to sin; and sin, when it is full-grown, gives birth to death."

But I'm impressed with the way Jesus himself handled the devil in the desert. Without exception, Jesus' response to the tempter was to quote Scripture. "It is written," he said again and again. "It is written." And I take it that Jesus was not only reminding the devil of the authority of God's Word, but reminding himself of what God expects from us on this earth.

A good antidote to temptation is a strong dose of Scripture, administered daily into the heart!

Along with this, Jesus' encounter with the devil suggests another antidote: It's letting the devil know in no uncertain terms what we are all about. Declaring to him our mission. Informing him of our game plan. For as long as the devil has reason to believe that we are clueless about our mission and game plan, and as long as he thinks we have no idea what we are about, then he operates upon the assumption that we are vulnerable to attack.

Today he can trick us into thinking that the "little white lie" we might tell is actually to someone's benefit. Tomorrow he can send someone into our life who, with but the slightest wink of the eye, can unleash a flood of sexual lust within us. And the next day he'll find something that makes us so angry that we vent our anger in some clearly sinful way, not just in "righteous indignation."

But if the devil knows that I have truly committed myself to being God's person, then he might—just might—leave me alone for awhile. Like any enemy, he prefers soft targets.

What the devil needs to hear from me is that, when it comes to my life, there is no such thing as a *God-forsaken* desert. The tempter needs to know unequivocally that, wherever I go, no matter how far away from my family and friends, I take God with me. He needs to know beyond a shadow of a doubt that, no matter how barren or foreboding my life may appear, I have *willed* that God should be at my side.

When the devil finds out that there is simply no way I'm going to be his man, the odds are he'll be tempted to take his bag of sleazy tricks elsewhere. The serendipity is that, if I can successfully persuade the devil that I'm exclusively God's person, then I will have successfully persuaded myself as well.

And at that point the devil's sordid game is *really* over!

Chapter Twenty-four

"Blessed are those

who are persecuted."

MATTHEW 5:10

Persecution

On what the Christian world recognizes as Good Friday, I found myself in Jerusalem in the midst of pilgrims from around the world thronging the narrow passages of the Via Dolorosa (the Way of Sorrows), hoping to walk in Jesus' footsteps from his judgment by Pilate to his crucifixion and burial.

Bearing crosses—some crude and wooden, some elaborate and covered with gold—the pilgrims followed one after another all day long. The processions seemed endless. To my amazement, there was even a unique procession formed by Arab Catholic Boy Scouts and Girl Scouts, dressed in the traditional Scouts uniforms.

Throughout the long day the air was filled with an incongruous mixture of hymn-singing and political tension. Because the Via Dolorosa winds its way mostly through the Muslim Quarter, Israeli police protecting the pilgrims were not just carrying guns on their shoulders as usual. Today their fingers were on the trigger. At one point I thought wisdom was the better part of valor and skirted around an angry group of Muslims who were protesting being refused entry into their own local territory because of the Good Friday processions.

At another point the police rudely forced a young Arab boy to turn his pastry cart around so as to get out of the way of an approaching group of pilgrims. I couldn't help but feel sorry for the boy, and wondered at the long-term repercussions of that small incident in his attitude toward the Israeli authorities and perhaps even in his view of Christianity. It wasn't much, but I hoped the coin of friendship I pressed into his hand as I walked by might have done something to soften the insult.

All in all, the sights and sounds along the Via Dolorosa were a mixture of reverence and revelry; of humble piety and flashy performance; of religious fervor and political resentment. It was a Kodak day, with cameras clicking and film crews vying for the best shots of both impromptu homage and organized pomp.

For each group of pilgrims it was a long, slow process, with mandatory stops at the 14 "stations of the cross." Most of the "stations" memorialize biblical events during Jesus' last hours, but at least five are the product of twelfth-century tradition.

The processions began at the first station (now a school), believed to be the Antonia Fortress of Pontius Pilate, where Jesus was condemned. Station two, across the road, is the Monastery of Flagellation, the supposed site where Jesus was scourged and burdened with the cross. A nearby archway over the Via Dolorosa marks the Convent of the Sisters of Zion, in the basement of which is a large cistern and Roman courtyard, a suggested site where Pilate might have presented Jesus, saying, "Behold the man!"

Stations three and four perpetuate the tradition that Jesus stumbled under the weight of the cross, and that Jesus' mother,

Mary, came out of the crowd to be with her son. At station five, a small chapel marks what is believed to be the spot where Simon from Cyrene was forced to help Jesus carry the cross.

The next two stations, six and seven, take pilgrims back to mere tradition, where it is said that a woman named Veronica stepped up to Jesus and wiped his face, and where Jesus was once again said to have fallen. But station eight references the factual biblical account where Jesus addressed the women of Jerusalem, saying, "Daughters of Jerusalem, do not weep for me; weep for yourselves and for your children."

After station nine (yet a third time where tradition has Jesus stumbling), the remaining stations are all within the Church of the Holy Sepulchre. At station ten Jesus is stripped of his garments; at station eleven he is nailed to the cross. Station twelve takes the pilgrim from the Catholic chapel to the Greek Orthodox chapel, where Jesus is thought to have been lifted up on the cross and died; and station thirteen is found in the Franciscan section, commemorating the taking down of Jesus' body.

The pilgrimage along the Via Dolorosa ends at station fourteen, where there is an elaborately decorated marble structure presented as being the tomb where Jesus' body was laid to rest. Although not specifically explained this way, presumably station fourteen also commemorates the *risen* Savior, without whose resurrection there would never have been processions along the Via Dolorosa these 20 centuries later.

Not being one for ecclesiastical hype—much less speculative tradition—I had mixed feelings about the day's events. On one hand, it was easy to believe that, because of all the hubbub going on, the events surrounding Jesus' last hours before his death were being trivialized rather than honored. (I even noticed that many of the monks in the various processions were themselves carrying cameras.) On the other hand, one would be hard-pressed to view this reenactment of the cross being borne up the narrow path to the most likely place of Jesus' crucifixion without being touched by the reality which lay beneath it.

What an incredible thought that on a given day in history, a day not unlike today, the Son of God bore his own cross to Calvary and died for me! Hallelujah, what a Savior!

So I'm glad I came when I came. To be reminded. To be deeply touched. Is there anything more challenging than the thought of truly "following in the footsteps of Jesus"? All day long the haunting words of Jesus kept ringing in my ears: "If anyone would come after me, he must deny himself and take up his cross daily and follow me."

Am I simply going through the motions of following Jesus without knowing what it means to be persecuted for my faith, or suffering indignities as a believer, or standing up for what I believe, no matter what the cost? What crosses have I taken up lately? If following in Jesus' footsteps means anything at all, surely it means identifying with Jesus in personal suffering, true submission, and genuine sacrifice.

As I look back on my life as a Christian, I wonder about the "stations" of my life as a Christian. If the many times I have stumbled are embarrassingly evident, when are the times that I have valiantly carried my cross? How have I really suffered as a Christian?

It's easy, of course, for me to say that I would be *willing* to suffer, if only my Christian faith were the object of some official or unofficial persecution. Yet because I live in two countries which happen to be remarkably free from religious abuse, my willingness to suffer is conveniently academic.

It's also easy to fool myself into thinking I have "suffered" when the most I have experienced is perhaps some demeaning comment about my faith; or being snubbed because of my beliefs; or having to forgo something I'd really like to do simply because faithfulness to my convictions won't permit it. What little I actually "suffer" as a Christian is closer akin to "suffering from a cold"—more of a nuisance than anything resembling martyrdom.

I also suspect that I don't have to suffer as a Christian because, as a Christian, I don't suffer nearly enough!

For example, how often does the kind of service I render to others *require* some suffering on my part? Do I render only that degree of service which, as David put it, "costs me nothing"?

When was the last time I was so aggressively evangelistic that I was kicked off the premises? Without actually intending it, am I not clever enough to calculate in advance just how far I can go in teaching others without risking any offense that might get me into trouble?

When it comes to giving, I like to believe that I'm generous, going out of my way at times to help others financially. But I have never once contributed so much to meet anyone's needs that my own creature comforts have been seriously threatened.

Worst of all, I can't honestly say that I've seriously sorrowed over the spiritual condition of those whom I believe to be lost in sin. Certainly I've prayed, and do pray, that they will come to Christ. And, yes, I even take the initiative in creating opportunities to teach others the good news of Jesus. But I don't weep over a sinful world as Jesus wept over a lost Jerusalem.

By what right, then, do I dare to walk in Jesus' footsteps along the Way of Sorrows? Is my life with Jesus merely a photo opportunity? Merely a token reenactment?

When I consider how far I have distanced myself from the suffering Messiah, it is a time for honest judgment and self-appraisal. The true Way of Sorrows is the pilgrimage of my own reluctant, woefully inadequate Christian witness. Self, not suffering, is the all-too-easy cross I bear.

At that thought I lift my shameful eyes and see before me the fifth station along the Via Dolorosa. But instead of Simon from Cyrene being compelled to help Jesus carry his cross, it is I who am being called to greater duty.

No, not by the ruthless Roman soldiers, but by one heart-wrenching glimpse of the Man of Sorrows, bloodied from a crown of thorns, and sweating under the weight of both his cross and mine.

Must Jesus bear the cross alone,
And all the world go free?
No, there's a cross for everyone,
And there's a cross for me.

—Thomas Shepherd

Chapter Twenty-five

"Let the fish

of the sea

inform you."

JOB 12:8

Stretching

There we were, sitting in a restaurant on the shore of the Sea of Galilee, eating St. Peter's fish and watching the boats which ply their way back and forth across that biblical "sea" (lake, really) which I had read about since childhood. I almost had to pinch myself to make sure I was really there.

Joseph always knows the best places to eat in Israel. I have to admit that, from its exterior appearance, I would never have picked this particular restaurant. But after a few words from Joseph to the kitchen staff, a sumptuous meal soon arrived at our table.

For starters, there was the usual *mensa*, or *hors d'oeuvres*, consisting of half a dozen or more little dishes which could be used as dips for the warm pita bread that was served. Then the fish arrived—grilled and still on the bone. *And with the head still attached!* So now I'm looking eyeball to eyeball with my lunch! Just when I think I've got the perfect solution—a paper napkin "shroud"—I look over at Joseph and see him eagerly digging into what I've just managed to cover up on my own plate. With his patented wicked smile, Joseph chided me for being so squeamish. "It's the best part of the fish!" he insisted. "Besides, it's very healthy." By this time we all knew that if Joseph said one of our meal selections was "very healthy," we could be sure it would be totally disgusting. (The grilled chicken hearts that he ordered for us earlier had been especially "healthy"!)

I'm fairly adventurous when it comes to trying new foods. (I did try the chicken hearts, but I wasn't impressed.) Yet I have to admit that my adventuresome spirit has its limits. There are times when even a burger with fries seems a preferable alternative.

I'm glad, though, that I tried the St. Peter's fish. It was mild, succulent, and delicious! But my curiosity was killing me: What were St. Peter's fish called when Peter himself was fishing them out of the Sea of Galilee?

Actually, in at least two ways Jesus himself is responsible for their present name. Had it not been for Jesus choosing Peter to be one of his apostles, probably no fish ever would have been named after him. What's more, had it not been for Jesus changing Simon's name to Peter, we likely would have been eating "*Simon's* fish" instead!

So why name a fish after Peter? Because Peter's life was inextricably tied to fishing—both for Galilee fish and for sinful men. And also because of his great faith.

Imagine for a moment that you are a Galilean fisherman cleaning your nets after being out on the water all night. An itinerant preacher comes along and asks if he can use your boat as a kind of floating pulpit to speak to the gathering crowd.

Then, at the end of his sermon, the preacher tells you to "put out into deep water, and let down the nets for a catch." But you explain that you've been out all night and have caught nothing. Under normal circumstances, that would have been the end of the matter. "Too bad," he might have said, and walked away. And you probably would turn to your fishing mates and say, "What a screwball! Who does he think he is?"

Yet Peter had a completely different response. (Was it prompted by something he heard Jesus say in his sermon?) Peter answered, "Master, we've worked hard all night and haven't caught anything. But because you say so, I will let down the nets." Now *there's* a sense of adventure for you! *There's* a willingness to try something different!

You already know what happens next. The catch of fish is so great that it threatens to sink the boat! More important, it's Simon Peter who gets hooked and becomes a faithful follower of Jesus. All because he was willing to *put out into the deep* as Jesus had told him to.

If there is anything that is hard for any of us, it is making the extra effort to *put out into the deep*. To be mentally and spiritually adventuresome. To stretch ourselves.

Most of us are content with the mediocre, the ordinary, and the humdrum. Mind you, there is nothing wrong with lives that are busy working, taking care of children, going shopping, or going to school. Life can't always, at every moment, be a boatfull of fish. Some days you throw out your line and nothing is biting.

Nor is it wrong to spend time making small talk about the day's events with the children, or about what happened at the office, or sports, or the weather. Sometimes I think God gave us weather so that we would never run out of something to say, particularly to those with whom we have very little else in common!

But sometimes small talk betrays that much of my life is spent in the shallows. What does it say about my life if my conversations are dominated with the kind of meal I had last night, or some television program I watched, or the "big game" that my team won or lost?

The older (and grumpier) I get, the more I think that, if God made the weather, the devil made sports. (I'm particularly convinced of that whenever the Super Bowl conflicts with a Sunday evening time of worship.) The devil doesn't have to get us to *renounce* our faith—only to be *distracted* from it by the trivial, the shallow, and the unworthy.

Sitting on the shore of the Sea of Galilee, I wondered how many people there in the town of Tiberias stopped each day to think about the miracles which had taken place in such close proximity to them. The lake which they are privileged to live by was the setting for some of the most incredible miracles Jesus ever performed. Wouldn't just knowing that fact provide special cause for pause as the sun rose over the sea each morning?

In my own mind's eye, I tried as hard as I could to visualize Jesus rebuking the winds and calming the sea. It was not hard to imagine the part about the storm. Just as Joseph had predicted at lunch, the winds blew up whitecaps on the water almost precisely from 3:30 to 4:30 in the afternoon. It happens virtually every day, as regular as clockwork.

Given that kind of headstart, all you have to do is to intensify what you're seeing until it becomes the "furious squall" that so panicked the disciples in the boat. Once you capture that image, you can't help but be amazed at the thought that Jesus "got up, rebuked the wind and said to the waves, 'Quiet! Be still!'" and instantly there was calm.

You can bet that the disciples who were with Jesus on that occasion were plenty impressed. "Who is this?" they asked. "Even the winds and the waves obey him!" And isn't that really the most profound question one can ever ask: *Who is Jesus?*

Jesus wasn't just *talking about* the weather, he was *controlling* it! Who but God himself, the Creator of the universe, could have done such a thing? Certainly it is something that no mere man could ever do. The local weatherman would never claim credit for it. No faith healer would dare attempt it. (*Pray* about the weather, perhaps, but not *rebuke it into submission!*)

In order to "put out into the deep," even those of us who are believers have to stretch ourselves to grasp the full implications of Jesus' miracles. Jesus wasn't just showing off when, on this same lake, he walked across the water and invited a trembling Peter to do the same. Remember that story?

Sending his disciples ahead of him by boat, Jesus stayed on the eastern side of the lake to pray. After the disciples had gone some three miles (about a third of the way across), they were once again worrying about a storm when suddenly they saw Jesus walking on the water! Peter made a brief attempt to walk toward Jesus, but lost faith and had to be hauled back into the boat.

On the surface, it's a nice story about faith and trust. Even children can understand that much. But is Jesus telling us nothing more than that by his power we too can do what seems to be impossible? For me, at least, the story once again raises that hauntingly deep question: *Who is Jesus? Who is this man who can walk on water?* It seems that Jesus himself was curious about our answer to that question. On one occasion he asked his disciples, "Who do people say the Son of Man is?" At first the disciples fudged, relaying to Jesus the local gossip. "Some say John the Baptist; others say Elijah; and still others, Jeremiah or one of the prophets."

But Jesus didn't want the small talk. He forced them out of the shallows of sensational checkout-counter headlines and into the deep waters of personal conviction. "But what about you?" he asked. "Who do you say I am?" (Can't you just see them looking at each other for moral support?)

Leave it to Peter to show the way. Hadn't Peter been the one to trust Jesus enough to "go out into the deep" in the first place? Hadn't Peter been the only disciple to even *try* to walk on the water?

Stepping up boldly, Simon Peter answered, "You are the Christ, the Son of the living God." To which Jesus responded, "Blessed are you, Simon son of Jonah, for this was not revealed to you by man, but by my Father in heaven. And I tell you that you are Peter, and on this rock I will build my church, and the gates of Hades will not overcome it."

If all that theological talk seems pretty deep, *it is!* The references to "Christ," "heavenly Father," "church," and "gates of Hades" lead us light-years away from small talk and humdrum lives. On the scale of eternity, our brief time on this earth must surely take on new urgency. How can we justify wasting so much precious time for nothing more than small talk?

In view of Hades (the unseen world of the afterlife), our purpose for even breathing takes on new meaning. How can we go on living out our routine lives so oblivious to the inevitability of death? How can we spend so much time on jobs, sports, or even families, and so little time with church-related matters, or praising Christ, or praying to our heavenly Father?

In the Person of Jesus—the One who filled Peter's boat with uncatchable fish, whose voice stilled the winds and the waves, and whose feet walked on water, is found all the answers to life.

If you want to be really adventuresome, leave the shallow life behind and "put out into the deep." What you may discover is that you'll have more than you ever need, that the storms in your life will be strangely calmed, and that, by taking the first step on the waters of faith, you can do things you never thought possible.

It's all about being spiritually adventurous. Better yet, about stretching. Straight into the arms of the man from Galilee.

> *While on the sea hear the terrible roaring;*
> *See how the boat of my life rolls with me;*
> *In fear of death and in deepest of anguish.*
> *Lord, hear my prayer, watch my soul on*
>   *the sea.*
>
> —*Anonymous Ukrainian Poem*
> *Translated by Stephan Bilak*

Chapter Twenty-six

"Get ready

to cross

the Jordan."

Joshua 1:2

Beginnings

It's just a river—a common, ordinary river. Unlike the great rivers of the world, the Jordan hasn't been a busy artery of commerce, or powered some important hydroelectric plant, or been the source of thriving civilizations (as, for example, the Nile or the Ganges). Yet because of its biblical associations, the Jordan River is one of the most famous rivers of all.

Springing from four sources near Mount Hermon in the north of Israel, the Jordan runs helter-skelter some 17 miles south to the Sea of Galilee, dropping dramatically more than 900 feet. Then, from the southern edge of the Galilee, the river meanders gently some 135 twisting miles before emptying into the Dead Sea.

Today, unfortunately, the visitor to Israel is unable to see much of the Jordan. Because the river flows within the security zone along Israel's eastern border, there is almost no access south of Galilee. Still, what little you *can* see of the Jordan more than sufficiently rewards any extra effort it takes to get there. For believers, the first glimpse of the Jordan is an emotional experience like few others.

It is like coming home. Like being connected. Like finding your roots.

For those who have been immersed in faith, the Jordan rekindles those first wonderful feelings of newness and forgiveness that accompany biblical faith and baptism. It was in the desert region of the Jordan that John the Baptizer came, "preaching a baptism of repentance for the forgiveness of sins." Penitent sinners from Jerusalem and all over the Judean countryside responded joyfully to his message. "Confessing their sins, they were baptized by him in the Jordan River."

One baptism was more special than all the rest. So special, in fact, that John himself was surprised by it. You can almost see John doing a doubletake as he is standing up to his waist in the Jordan, wet all over from already having baptized scores of people that morning. Turning to invite the next person in line to come down into the water, John suddenly recognizes the face. It's Jesus! Confused, and undoubtedly somewhat embarrassed, John says to Jesus, "I need to be baptized by you, and do you come to me?"

As John well knew, his baptism was a matter of repentance and forgiveness of sins. That being the case, it made no sense for the sinless Son of God to be immersed along with the crowd of sinners there that day. Unlike them, Jesus had no need for repentance or forgiveness.

But Jesus insisted, saying, "It is proper for us to do this to fulfill all righteousness." It's as if Jesus felt the need to do himself whatever he would be asking others to do. He had to be an example. He had to lead the way. Once John realized why Jesus had come, he dispatched his doubts and immersed him.

Can you imagine what it would be like, not just to see Jesus face-to-face, but to actually stand with him there in the water and immerse the sinless Son of God? It's something like that feeling, I think, that is part of what you experience as you stand on the banks of the Jordan today and realize that our Lord's own baptism was in that very river.

Somehow, mystically, you become a witness to his baptism, as he has been a witness to yours.

So the Jordan is inextricably linked with baptism. You can hardly think of one without the other. Jordan; baptism. Baptism; Jordan. No wonder so many pilgrims come to Israel to be baptized in its waters—not because the water itself is holy, but because the river links us so closely in memory to him who made our forgiveness possible.

Yet the Jordan is also inextricably linked with new beginnings. (Baptism itself is a new beginning!) Flip back through your Bible, and you will see any number of times when the Jordan was the focal point of quite extraordinary beginnings. For example, when Jacob was returning to Canaan after being in Haran for many years, he reflected back on how richly blessed he had been during that time. He had left with virtually nothing but had come back with flocks and herds and a retinue of children and servants (which, for tactical reasons, he had divided into two groups).

Therefore Jacob thanks God for the new life which he was given beyond the Jordan. "I am unworthy of all the kindness and faithfulness you have shown your servant," says Jacob. "I had only my staff when I crossed this Jordan, but now I have become two groups." For Jacob, crossing the Jordan meant a transformation from nothing to something; from insecurity to security; from failure to success.

The Jordan was also associated with two prophets: Elijah and his young protégé, Elisha. When the time came for God to take

Elijah, the two prophets walked from Jericho to the Jordan. There, on the western bank, Elijah "took his cloak, rolled it up and struck the water with it."

Like the parting of the Red Sea, the waters of the Jordan divided, allowing the two men to walk across on the dry riverbed. After Elijah was caught up to heaven in a whirlwind, Elisha took Elijah's cloak and repeated the miraculous crossing from the east bank back to the west.

What an exciting beginning to Elisha's ministry! And how truly prophetic it was in its symbolism. Just as Elisha began his ministry by being "baptized" in the waters of the Jordan, so too would Jesus begin his ministry in those same waters.

I simply love the parallels. When Elisha crossed back through the Jordan, a group of prophets who had witnessed the miracle said, "The spirit of Elijah is resting on Elisha." When Jesus came up out of the water after being baptized, "he saw the Spirit of God descending like a dove and lighting on him." And when Peter told the first believers on Pentecost to repent and be baptized, he promised that they too would receive not only the forgiveness of sin but "the gift of the Holy Spirit"!

Jordan; baptism. Baptism; Jordan. Baptism; Holy Spirit. Holy Spirit; baptism. Baptism; new beginning. New beginning; baptism.

Then, of course, there is Naaman, the Syrian army commander who was healed of his leprosy after first snubbing, then obeying, Elisha's directions to wash himself seven times in the Jordan. It was one occasion when not just any river would do. In his anger that Elisha didn't come out and wave a magic wand like he had expected, Naaman was about to leave Israel in a huff. "Are not Abana and Pharpar, the rivers of Damascus, better than any of the waters of Israel?" he sneered. "Couldn't I wash in them and be cleansed?"

Fortunately, his servants reminded him of what a little thing he was being asked to do, and so he did it. What a thrill it must have been to have dipped six times, then seven, and come up out of the water with skin "clean like that of a young boy." It was like being reborn!

Had Dougie Brown's prayerful chorus been written at the time, I suspect that Naaman would have been singing it in his chariot over and over again, all the way back to Damascus.

> *River, wash over me,*
> *Cleanse me and make me new.*
> *Bathe me, refresh me and fill me anew.*
> *River, wash over me.*

If you know anything at all about the history of Israel, you will know that I have omitted until now one of the most significant references to the Jordan in all of the Bible. It comes when the Israelites cross the Jordan into the long-awaited Promised Land. Just as Elijah and Elisha crossed the Jordan on dry land, some six centuries earlier the entire nation of Israel had made its own miraculous crossing. "As soon as the priests who carried the ark reached the Jordan and their feet touched the water's edge, the water from upstream stopped flowing."

For Israel, crossing the Jordan meant going from the arid desert of their wilderness wanderings into a land "flowing with milk and honey." It meant all the difference between slavery and freedom. It meant having a lasting possession, not just temporary ties to a land not their own. It meant hope. Inheritance. Salvation. Peace. Love. It meant a new beginning.

I've saved this reference till last because it speaks of the greatest new beginning that you and I can ever have: our own personal entrance into the Promised Land of life eternal. The next Jordan you and I will cross will lead us into a realm we can scarcely imagine. I don't know if "milk and honey" does anything for you, or even a "street made of pure gold," but there's no way we could miss the message of such figurative language: What's on the other side is too good to miss! Heaven won't be a disappointment to anyone!

But first there is that river to cross. That Jordan of death which we so much fear. Who was it that said, "Everybody wants to go to heaven, but nobody wants to die"? Yet death and life eternal come as a package. No Jordan, no Promised Land.

When I think of that pairing, I can't help but think of the slaves on the American plantations. Facing death in a way that most of us never will—each day for a lifetime—they came to see death not as an enemy to be avoided at all cost but as a welcome friend. No wonder they sang about the Jordan, a river in a faraway land which they would never see. No wonder they associated the Jordan with freedom and promise and hope and joy.

For them, death was a crossing to be eagerly anticipated. For them, death meant the only chance they would ever have for a new beginning. Just listen to them singing in the cotton fields, backs aching, hearts filled with pain:

> *Swing low, sweet chariot,*
> *Comin' for to carry me home.*
> *Swing low, sweet chariot,*
> *Comin' for to carry me home.*

I looked over Jordan and what did I see?
Comin' for to carry me home?
A band of angels, comin' after me,
Comin' for to carry me home.

Do you and I—far from cotton fields and slavery—have anything like the kind of hopeful expectation the slaves had for death? Can we in all honesty sing their sentiments?

When I think of the Jordan of my own death, I'm not sure I'm all that excited about crossing it. But it does help to know that I've already stood on its banks and symbolically gone down into its waters in baptism. Once in the water, why not cross over?

In his classic hymn, *Guide Me, O Thou Great Jehovah*, William Williams draws strength from Jordan's symbolism in this masterful verse about the fear and anxiety of facing death:

When I tread the verge of Jordan,
Bid my anxious fears subside;
Bear me through the swelling current,
Land me safe on Canaan's side;
Songs of praises
I will ever give to Thee.

For me, it also helps to know that so many have gone on ahead: Jacob, the Israelites, Elijah and Elisha, Naaman, John the Baptizer, Jesus—and my own father in the flesh. They have all now crossed the Jordan to the other side. And if they all found the Promised Land, so will I. Having already been plunged beneath the water, why should I now fear the baptism of death? It is not the end, only the beginning!

On Jordan's stormy banks I stand,
And cast a wishful eye
To Canaan's fair and happy land,
Where my possessions lie.
I am bound for the promised land,
I am bound for the promised land;
O who will come and go with me?
I am bound for the promised land.

—Samuel Stennett

Chapter Twenty-seven

"Guard your heart,

for it is

the wellspring of life."

PROVERBS 4:23

Perspective

Maybe I've just seen too many mountains. Maybe I'm comparing it with the Golan Heights west of the Galilee, or the 9000-foot Mount Hermon further north. But the Mount of Beatitudes isn't even close to what I had expected to see. It's more like a hill. A low hill.

Yet if you are a resident of Tiberias or Capernaum on the Sea of Galilee and look up to the 330-foot summit of the hill, perhaps it seems like a "mountain."

Perspective: It depends upon where you are at the time. The location of the observer determines the observation.

Or maybe it depends upon what you are accustomed to. If you have never seen the Atlantic or Pacific Ocean, a big lake might seem like a "sea" to you. Hence, I suppose, the "Sea of Galilee" rather than "Lake Galilee."

Perspective: Whatever you get used to has a way of becoming the norm. If you've never *seen* it another way, how can you *imagine* it another way?

So there I was on the top of the Mount of Beatitudes for the very first time, feeling a strange mixture of exhilaration and disappointment. *Exhilaration* at simply being there in that historic spot. *Disappointment* that what I had expected to be a spectacular mountain was little more than an ordinary hill. How could I have been so mistaken?

Perspective: Personally being there always gives one a greater appreciation for that which may have been known about, but never experienced.

As I think about it, my disappointment in seeing the Mount of Beatitudes for the first time may well have been a special blessing. After all, isn't that what the Mount of *Beatitudes* is all about—*blessings*? "Blessed are the poor in spirit," said Jesus in his so-called Sermon on the Mount. "Blessed are those who mourn." "Blessed are the meek."

Now that I've been to the scene of his sermon, I can't help but think, "Blessed, too, are those who gain true perspective." Not just about the mountain, but also about life!

There I was on the Mount of Beatitudes, thinking about *physical* perspective, when I began reading the Sermon on the Mount. Suddenly I was sure I heard Jesus talking about *spiritual* perspective. Isn't that what his sermon was all about? Isn't that what you and I—looking at the world through our finite human spectacles—have such difficulty grasping?

Even the overture to the sermon tells us that the meaning of life is anything but what we've always thought it to be. The poor, the meek, the hungry, and those who mourn are supposed to be *happy*? Humanly speaking, does that make any sense?

And does it ring true that I'm supposed to love my enemies? If I loved them, they wouldn't be my enemies, would they? Nor do I naturally resonate with "turning the other cheek." Run away, maybe; restrain myself from retaliation, perhaps; but not turn my cheek and beg for more!

Oddly enough, "doing unto others what I would have them do to me" sounds a bit more palatable. At the very least, it has a patina of self-interest. But how then can I possibly take seriously Jesus' teaching that "if anyone takes what belongs to you, do not demand it back"?

Since I don't believe I have the right to keep something that I've taken from someone else, I hardly see how the "do unto others" principle can work in such an instance. Recognizing *their* right to take back from me what is theirs surely implies *my* right to take back what is mine. Taken together, can those two principles possibly make sense?

In his remarkable sermon, Jesus takes us beyond *perspective* to *paradox*. To self-contradiction. To the seemingly absurd!

That mournful people should be happy makes no earthly sense. Loving one's enemies makes no earthly sense. Turning the other cheek makes no earthly sense. And giving to anyone who asks—whether in need or out of sheer greed—certainly makes no earthly sense. I'm telling you, the Sermon on the Mount seems absolutely, unqualifiedly absurd!

It seems absurd in our eyes, because there is a clash between how you and I view things and how God views things. Talk about your "spectacular mountain views"! What could be more spectacular—or more perceptive—than a view of the world from heaven's window! No wonder Jeremiah said, "It is not for man to direct his steps."

It is not altogether unlike the difference in perspective between myself and the pesky fly who can't figure out that I've opened the window right next to him so that he can escape! Or the perspective of an adult, as compared with that of a child, when it comes to recognizing impending danger.

Perspective: Who could have more of it than the God who created us, and who has revealed his mind to us so that we could both recognize impending spiritual danger and take advantage of the many "windows of escape" which he has opened for us?

What Jesus teaches in his Sermon on the Mount takes us from the known to the unknown, from the deceptively familiar to a whole new realm of spiritual insight. Indeed, from the human to the divine. Jesus pulls and tugs at our world and turns it inside out!

As I looked over the Mount of Beatitudes on a lovely spring day, I saw all around me "lilies of the field"—the delicate flowers that grace the mountain in the springtime. Jesus didn't just see the flowers, he shared with us their fragrant message about the futility of worry. And flying here and there from tree to bush and back again were any number of birds—on whose wings, so it seems, Jesus was trying to teach us the joy of simple trust:

> *Therefore I tell you, do not worry about your life,*
> *what you will eat or drink; or about your body, what*
> *you will wear. Is not life more important than food,*
> *and the body more important than clothes?*

> *Look at the birds of the air; they do not sow or reap*
> *or store away in barns, and yet your heavenly Father*
> *feeds them. Are you not much more valuable than*
> *they? Who of you by worrying can add a single hour*
> *to his life?*

And why do you worry about clothes? See how the lilies of the field grow. They do not labor or spin. Yet I tell you that not even Solomon in all his splendor was dressed like one of these. If that is how God clothes the grass of the field, which is here today and tomorrow is thrown into the fire, will he not much more clothe you, O you of little faith? . . .

Therefore do not worry about tomorrow, for tomorrow will worry about itself. Each day has enough trouble of its own.

Worry is nothing more than a lack of perspective—and a lack of faith in him who has perfect perspective.

But the Sermon on the Mount is more than just a matter of positioning one's self into a proper perspective. It is a call for getting to the core of life's meaning. For moving beyond the external to the internal. For discovering the heart of the matter. For appreciating the distinction between *doing* and *being*.

Listen again as Jesus takes us from *action* to *thought*, from *hands* to *heart*: "You have heard that it was said to the people long ago, 'Do not murder, and anyone who murders will be subject to judgment.' But I tell you that anyone who is angry with his brother will be subject to judgment."

Just when we thought we could condemn the murderer and look good by comparison, Jesus shakes us from our moral smugness and gives us a whole new perspective on who we are. In our anger, we too have become murderers!

And just when we thought that our citizenship in the kingdom of heaven was safely moored to our religious beliefs or our involvement in some church activity, Jesus brings us up short, saying sharply, "Many will say to me on that day, 'Lord, Lord, did we not prophesy in your name, and in your name drive out demons and perform many miracles?' Then I will tell them plainly, 'I never knew you. Away from me, you evildoers!'"

The heart of the matter is that man looks on the outside, but God looks on the inside. "The LORD does not look at the things man looks at," God told Samuel. "Man looks at the outward appearance, but the LORD looks at the heart."

If it weren't for acknowledging God's exclusive insight into the inner man, we could scarcely make sense of what seem to be screaming contradictions in Jesus' sermon. For example, Jesus says, "Do not judge, or you too will be judged," then he turns right around and encourages us to judge false prophets, saying "by their fruit you will recognize them." What else can this mean but that we have the ability to judge a person's actions, but not his heart?

And how, apart from God's focus on the heart, can we possibly reconcile Jesus' earlier instruction, "Let your light shine before men, that they may see your good deeds and praise your Father in heaven," with his later instruction, "Be careful not to do your 'acts of righteousness' before men, to be seen by them"? God wants us to practice righteous deeds, but only for the advancement of the kingdom, not for our own glory.

Again, the heart of the matter is a matter of the *heart*. It's what's in the heart that makes the real difference in life.

The difference between external righteousness and internal righteousness is all the difference between the Mount of Beatitudes and Mount Everest! And yet I keep getting the two confused. I keep thinking and acting as if it's what I do on the outside that really counts, not who I am on the inside. I've got *doing* and *being* mixed up. Sometimes *doing* is important. More often, it's *being* that counts.

Of course I am not alone in my warped perspective of values, priorities, and commitments. It seems that human nature itself is wrapped in a veil of ignorance about what is real and unreal, about what is genuine and what is counterfeit. Everywhere I turn, the world is saying to me that what Jesus taught on that little slope in Galilee is absurd.

Yet whatever the world thinks, I'm convinced it is not Jesus' teaching that is absurd. Rather, it is my own flawed human perspective which is in fuzzy focus. I am the one who is out of touch with reality, not Jesus. I am the one who gets life so completely and utterly backward. It is my life that is so truly paradoxical—so embarrassingly inconsistent and absurd!

Just imagine my thinking that this life is so ultimately important that I spend my time trying to accumulate wealth here on earth rather than preparing for a life where I'll have more treasure than I could ever hope to enjoy! Just imagine my worrying about what's going to happen to me next year, when I'm not even guaranteed tomorrow! Just imagine my thinking that, if I can fool most of the people most of the time, I can also fool God!

What I need is a new perspective on life. The difference between a mountain and a hill is merely a matter of altitude. One is higher, the other is lower. But the difference between a meaningless life and one that truly makes sense is a matter of *attitude*. Or, as Jesus taught, our *be*-attitudes.

Dear Lord and Father of mankind,
Forgive our foolish ways!
Re-clothe us in our rightful mind,
In purer lives Thy service find,
In deeper reverence, praise.

—John Greenleaf Whittier

Chapter Twenty-eight

"Learn to revere

the LORD your God."

DEUTERONOMY 14:23

Reverence

W hat's wrong with this picture? Look at any panoramic photo of Jerusalem, and what stands out as the city's most spectacular landmark is the golden-domed, blue-tiled, octagonal Dome of the Rock. For both Christians and Jews, there must surely be a grand irony at work. Of all the "holy places" in Jerusalem, the one most visible, and most symbolic of the Holy City, is neither Jewish nor Christian, but Muslim.

Towering above both the Church of the Holy Sepulchre and the Wailing Wall, the Dome of the Rock imposes the imprint of Islam on Jerusalem by its sheer size. And also by its sheer beauty. The golden dome (actually a bronze-aluminum alloy) is absolutely resplendent. The mosque itself is neatly situated in a lovely parklike setting on Temple Mount, along with the adjacent, less elaborate El Aqsa Mosque.

In the latter, the stained-glass windows and exquisite Oriental rugs provide the focal points, while in the former, the underside of the golden dome arrests your attention. On the ceiling is magnificent gilded design work, richly accented in deep scarlet. In contrast to the gaudiness and eclectic architecture in most of the Christian shrines I have seen, the dignified simplicity of the mosque is refreshing. No animal or human images here. Only floral or geometrical designs, or verses from the Koran written on the walls in elaborate (typically gilded) Arabic script.

What distinguishes the Dome of the Rock from other mosques I have visited is the centerpiece which gives rise to its name: the huge rock around which the mosque was constructed. To Muslims, it is the rock from which Muhammad had his famous Night Ride. By Muslim tradition, Muhammad was awakened from his sleep by the Archangel Gabriel, and was whisked away from Mecca on a winged horse to "the far distant Place of Worship" (said to be Temple Mount). There, from on top of the rock, Muhammad and the winged horse ascended through the seven heavens and met Allah, before returning to Mecca with God's commandments for the faithful in hand.

Muslims are not the only ones with traditions surrounding the rock. Considered to be the summit of Mount Moriah, the rock is also venerated as the site of Abraham's near-sacrifice of his son Isaac. It is also believed (with more historical basis) to be the site of Araunah's threshing floor, on which King David built the altar of repentance after ordering the census of Israel against God's wishes.

If, in fact, the rock is to be associated with Araunah's threshing floor and David's altar, then it was upon this very site that Solomon built the temple. Hence, Temple Mount. Hence, too, the political football which the rock and the area surrounding it have become down through the centuries. Who ever would have thought that something as cold and lifeless as a rock could be the source of such religious veneration and political conflict?

Two things in particular stood out. One is the "no shoes" rule. Before entering the mosques, visitors are required to take off their shoes and leave them outside. (I couldn't help but wonder if shoes—or cameras, which are also prohibited—ever went missing!) Undoubtedly, this practice can be traced back to Moses and the burning bush, when God said to Moses, "Take off your sandals, for the place where you are standing is holy ground."

While I disagree with Muslims about their mosques literally being on holy ground, I very much appreciate their "sense of place" when it comes to worshiping. I sometimes wonder if we who are Christians have lost that "sense of place" as we worship, whether individually or congregationally. If the house of worship itself is not holy (and it is not), you can be sure that time spent worshiping in the presence of Jehovah God is indeed "holy ground."

The second thing that always impresses me about Muslim worship is the emphasis given to prayer—both in its frequency (five times each day) and in its form. When Muslims pray, they get down on their knees and bow their faces to the ground.

As for the frequency, I confess that I lag far behind in my own regular prayers. Although I maintain an informal, ongoing dialogue of prayer throughout each day, I also realize that my prayers are enhanced when I quite literally stop everything I'm doing and offer praise and prayer to God. It is all the difference between having a conversation with someone in another room and earnestly talking face-to-face.

As for the form of praying—whether sitting, standing, raising hands, or kneeling—I've always felt that it didn't really matter. What matters is that our minds and hearts are in the right position: focused and sincere. But, the more I think about it, the more I wonder. If body language can often tell us many things about a person's inner thoughts, then perhaps there is something more to be considered about how we position ourselves when we pray.

Everywhere I look around me, I see more and more believers raising their hands during a time of prayer, and especially during songs of praise. And, certainly, raising hands is biblical. Did not the apostle Paul say, "I want men everywhere to lift up holy hands in prayer, without anger or disputing"? But, as with any form of worship, raising hands can have its own problems. Is the practice spontaneous or orchestrated? Heartfelt or habit? A genuine expression of praise or merely trendy?

Each of these questions, of course, could be asked of those who pray while sitting, standing, kneeling, or bowing. In the human heart there is always the battle between form and substance. Yet I find it intriguing that, in current culture, raising hands is quite acceptable—even popular—while there is little or no evidence that praying while kissing the ground has yet caught on.

That observation becomes all the more intriguing when one considers the number of times the Bible refers to people of faith bending the knee, or bowing (not just their heads, but their entire bodies), or falling facedown to the ground while praying. For example, the psalmist says, "Come, let us bow down in worship, let us kneel before the LORD our Maker." (An equal number of passages warn against bowing down to other gods.)

In a lesser known passage than the one about Moses and the burning bush, we discover precedent for both the Muslim rule regarding "no shoes" and the practice of bowing facedown to the ground as a matter of reverence. The passage records what happened when Joshua was suddenly confronted by an angel who identified himself as "the commander of the LORD's army":

> Then Joshua fell facedown to the ground in reverence, and asked him, "What message does my Lord have for his servant?" The commander of the LORD's army replied, "Take off your sandals, for the place where you are standing is holy." And Joshua did so.

When was the last time you or I expressed reverence for God by falling facedown to the ground? Indeed, when was the last time we expressed respect for *anyone* by falling facedown to the ground?

In instance after instance in Scripture, we see respect and reverence being shown by means of bowing facedown. Ruth bowed with her face to the ground before Boaz; as did David to Absalom; and David to Saul; and Abigail to David; and Saul to Samuel; and Araunah to David; and Bathsheba to David. Providing the ultimate example, Jesus himself—in Gethsemane—prayed to his heavenly Father while lying prostrate with his face to the ground.

It would be easy, of course, to dismiss this kind of bowing as merely cultural, and therefore historically passé. Yet I can't help but wonder if bowing in obeisance has gone out of style for another cultural reason: because we, in our culture, bow to no one. Because we are too proud to get down on our knees as a sign of humility and respect. Because bowing suggests the kind of submission which we have all been conditioned to reject.

If perhaps raising our hands fits comfortably with our cultural commitment to excitement and celebration, bowing to anyone or anything in an era of unprecedented rights, choice, and self-esteem could not be more uncomfortable.

But therein lies my own dilemma. If I am unwilling to prostrate myself before God, how can I hope to ever worship him? After all, that is what the word *worship* means: to kiss toward, to prostrate one's self in homage. If there is a time to raise my hands in praise, there is also a time for me to fall facedown to the ground in reverence before God.

The shame of it all is that I am prompted in these reflections on worship by people of faith who bow their knees, not to Jesus Christ, but to Muhammad. They have built their mosque over a meaningless rock, while Jesus said, "On this rock I will build my church." Of course, the "rock" of which Jesus spoke was not a "sacred rock" on Temple Mount, but the singular truth that he is the one sovereign Prophet of God, "the Christ, the Son of the living God."

But how very easy it is for me to point out the grievous error of Muslims when they kiss the ground toward Mecca and Muhammad, while I fail so miserably to show the reverence which is due to the One who is Lord over all, even over Muhammad. If I have something to teach the Muslim on his prayer mat, I also have something to learn.

For the day of the Lord is coming when "at the name of Jesus every knee will bow, in heaven and on earth and under the earth, and every tongue confess that Jesus Christ is Lord, to the glory of God the Father." Unlike the Muslim, I have already confessed the name of Jesus. But how will I feel on that Great Day when at last I meet him in person? Will it be the first time he has seen me on my knees at his feet? Will I fall down awkwardly in an unfamiliar position of reverence? To say the least, now would be a good time to practice.

I am not so naive as to believe that reverence for God requires my nose being constantly in the dust, or my lips being permanently pressed against a prayer rug. Whether I am looking up or down, whether north or south, east or west, my prayers still wing their way to heaven.

But I must never again tread so casually on holy ground. I must never again enter into a time of worship with a contemporary familiarity that breeds contempt. Nor dare I raise my hands in joyful praise without falling to my knees in humble submission to God's will in my life.

If the picture of Jerusalem today seems desecrated by a resplendent monument to a false prophet, there is another picture of Jerusalem—the heavenly Jerusalem—that is far more resplendent. In words painted on the broadest possible canvas, the writer of Hebrews brings us to our knees with a reminder of the sublime blessings which we have received in the unshakable kingdom of God. Are there more moving words in all of Scripture?

But you have come to Mount Zion, to the heavenly Jerusalem, the city of the living God. You have come to thousands upon thousands of angels in joyful assembly, to the church of the firstborn, whose names are written in heaven. You have come to God, the judge of all men, to the spirits of righteous men made perfect, to Jesus the mediator of a new covenant, and to the sprinkled blood that speaks a better word than the blood of Abel. . . .

Therefore, since we are receiving a kingdom that cannot be shaken, let us be thankful, and so worship God acceptably with reverence and awe, for our "God is a consuming fire."

Chapter Twenty-nine

"You were bought

at a price."

1 CORINTHIANS 7:23

Bargaining

Try as you might, it is virtually impossible to get around in the Old City of Jerusalem without walking through the labyrinth of narrow alleyways that comprise the *souk*, or marketplace. If you enter through the Jaffa Gate, you find yourself on the touristy David Street, where you are greeted by slogan-emblazoned T-shirts, cheap local jewelry, and even hats with solar-powered fans to keep you cool in the heat of Jerusalem summers.

But if you enter through the Damascus Gate, you find women sitting on the ground with their garden produce spread all around in a colorful splash of onions, tomatoes, lettuce, and other varieties of local vegetables.

Regardless of how you enter, once inside there is simply no end to the sights, sounds, and smells of the marketplace. Narrow stalls are packed with dried fruits, pastries, nuts, and more spices than you've ever seen in your life! Halfway up one of the alleyways I discovered what has to be the world's smallest cobbler shop (no more than four feet wide) with an old Singer sewing machine that reminded me of one my grandmother used to have.

At another stall I felt like a kid in a candy store. In fact, it *was* a candy store, and I can still see the smile of delight on a little Arab boy's face as he handed the merchant his two small coins, just as I used to do at a little corner grocery when I was his age.

Turning down another alley, I soon sensed both sights and smells that made the throat gag and the stomach retch. It was "butchers' row." After years of travel, I'm accustomed to seeing carcasses hanging up in outdoor markets. But I still haven't gotten used to exposed entrails and all manner of body parts best left undescribed. It was a relief to finally find my way back into the more touristy area near David Street.

The trade-off was having to endure all the hawkers. "Take a look. It costs you nothing," says one merchant while waving you into his stall. "Let's make a deal!" cries another. There is also the inevitable, "You're my first customer for the day, so special price. I make nothing!" The sales pitches and corny catchphrases come fast and furious.

When some item does catch your attention and you dare to venture inside one of the stalls, the bargaining begins. I don't have much heart for bargaining. Every fiber in my body wants to say, "Just give me your best price, and I'll gladly pay it." But if you give in to such timid instincts, you'll end up paying outrageous prices. So you play the game.

Rules of engagement include the following: Don't show too much interest in your prize. Look at other items so as not to focus too much on what you really want. Find every fault you can in the merchandise—and mumble aloud about it. Set a limit in your own mind which you absolutely will not go beyond. Make your starting bid at half what you are willing to pay. When your first offer is rejected, begin walking out of the stall. (Don't worry, they'll not let you walk away without a counteroffer!)

For the merchants of the Middle East, bargaining is a way of life. Even little children quickly learn the intricate art. No deal, it seems, is honorable unless there has been some spirited haggling in the process. And don't worry about offending sensitivities. No offense is taken when you play the game; in fact, offense is likely to be taken if you don't!

Indeed, bargaining is a time-honored tradition. In the Bible there are two wonderful examples of bargaining, both involving Abraham. One instance (which I find utterly amusing) takes place when Abraham is wanting to buy a burial plot for Sarah upon her death. When he approaches the Hittites living in Hebron and asks to purchase the cave of Machpelah from Ephron son of Zohar, you'd think Ephron was willing to just *give* Abraham the cave. "Listen to me," says Ephron; "I give you the field, and I give you the cave that is in it."

Abraham protests, saying, "Listen to me, if you will. I will pay the price of the field." But Ephron answers with all the shrewdness of a great bargainer: "The land is worth four hundred shekels of silver, but what is that between me and you? Bury your dead." (Can't you just see the sincerity dripping from his face!) And immediately, the text says, "Abraham agreed to Ephron's terms and weighed out for him the price he had named in the hearing of the Hittites."

Don't you love it? The price had been established by an (intentional) passing reference to the value of the "gift" Ephron was "giving" to Abraham! Both parties were playing a game. Both parties knew it. And both parties came away happy.

The second instance in which we find Abraham bargaining takes place at an earlier time, and the party with whom Abraham bargains is none other than God himself. Perhaps you'll recall Abraham's attempt to save the wicked city of Sodom, where Abraham's nephew Lot was living. Abraham appeals to God's mercy, saying, "Will you sweep away the righteous with the wicked? What if there are fifty righteous people in the city? Will you really sweep it away and not spare the place for the sake of the fifty righteous people in it?"

God readily agrees: "If I find 50 righteous people in the city of Sodom, I will spare the whole place for their sake." But Abraham apparently knows that finding even 50 righteous folks in Sodom is asking too much. So he speaks up again: "Now that I have been so bold as to speak to the Lord, though I am nothing but dust and ashes, what if the number of the righteous is five less than fifty? Will you destroy the whole city because of five people?" And God patiently says, "If I find forty-five there, I will not destroy it."

From 45, Abraham bargains with God down to 20. Then he says, "May the Lord not be angry, but let me speak just once more. What if only ten can be found there?" At this point God must surely be exasperated with Abraham; nevertheless, God answers, "For the sake of ten, I will not destroy it."

Apparently the point of all this bargaining was to show both God's graciousness and the extent of Sodom's wickedness. When God finally destroyed Sodom, it wasn't as if he hadn't given the people of Sodom every benefit of the doubt. At some point, however, God simply had no more room to bargain. At some point, justice demanded its due.

It makes me think about all the bargaining I've done with God. How many times have I said, "God, if you'll only let me get out of this embarrassing situation, I'll never do it again"? Or, "God, if you'll allow me just a little more time, I'll get my act together and do what I know is right." Or, "God, if you'll give me this or that, then I'll never ask for another thing!"

Do you find yourself making similar attempts at bargaining with God? When it comes to dealing with our heavenly Father, we all seem to revert to the cunning manipulation of our childhood.

Yet there are even more subtle forms of bargaining. I think, for example, of the would-be disciple who attempted to bargain with Jesus before committing himself fully to the Lord. I say "bargain," but he actually made what seemed to be a reasonable request: "Lord, first let me go and bury my father."

Jesus' surprising response sounds as unsympathetic as it would seem to be impossible. "Let the dead bury their own dead," said Jesus, "but you go and proclaim the kingdom of God."

If it were anyone else but Jesus, we might be tempted to say that his response was petty and uncaring. My guess, however, is that Jesus knew there was more than an act of bereavement standing in the man's way. Burying his father was only an excuse. What the man was really doing was bargaining for more time.

I've heard some people say, "I want to become a Christian, but I'm not good enough yet"; or, even more brashly, "I want to sow my wild oats before I become a Christian—so that I'll be a better Christian when I finally take that step." If the former is perhaps well-intended, the latter is hopelessly misguided! It is a shameful attempt to bargain with God, to make a deal on one's own terms, dependent upon one's own agenda.

Whether it be brazen bargaining of this type, or my own (seemingly more benign) form of negotiating, the bottom line is always the same: *We don't want to pay full price*. We want salvation and forgiveness and mercy at a cut-rate, bargain price. If it doesn't cost us too much, *maybe* we'll make a change in our lives. If it's "on sale," *maybe* we'll make a commitment to God. What a different attitude King David had when he was negotiating with Araunah the Jebusite to buy his threshing floor as a place to erect an altar to God! Araunah offered to give David the land and even the oxen for the burnt offerings, but David replied, "No, I insist on paying the full price. I will not take for the LORD what is yours, or sacrifice a burnt offering that costs me nothing."

When it comes to serving God, it is no time to be bargaining. God is not a used-car salesman. The irony is that God knows that we could never pay full price—or even half-price, for that matter. No amount of bargaining on our part could ever atone for our sins. That's why he *gave* us the sacrifice. That's why he sent his own Son into the world.

And that brings me back to the smelliest, most offensive part of the souk—"butchers' row." But first we need to clear the air about some traditional assumptions regarding Jesus' last hours before his crucifixion.

The chronology of events from the "last supper" onward is all a bit complicated, but John's Gospel tells us that Jesus was crucified on "the day of Preparation, and the next day was to be a special Sabbath." John also tells us that, on the morning after the "last supper," the Jews did not enter Pilate's palace because "they wanted to be able to eat the Passover."

In other words, despite Jesus' own comment regarding the Passover at the "last supper" ("I have eagerly desired to eat this Passover with you before I suffer"), it appears that his reference was more anticipatory than actual. If that is the case, and if the actual Passover meal was to be eaten at the end of the day upon which Jesus was crucified, then we see the most amazing thing happening: Jesus did not *eat* the Passover lamb; he *became* the Passover lamb— at precisely the same hour as the lambs in Jerusalem were being slaughtered and sold for the feast!

And this is where we find ourselves back in "butchers' row." Try to imagine it: After a sham trial before the Jewish Sanhedrin, and after hours of humiliation at the hands of Pilate and his Roman soldiers, Jesus is finally led out to be crucified. But what does he pass by along the way? What does Jesus see on the way to the cross?

A good guess is that Jesus was led through the souk on his way out of the city. If so, he must have seen a busy marketplace, with last-minute shoppers hurrying to get home before sundown. He must have seen the women with their vegetables, and the cobbler, and the candy man. But what must Jesus have thought when they led him down "butchers' row"? There were the lambs, hanging freshly butchered and bleeding, a final vivid reminder of the cruel death he was about to face as the Lamb of God.

What I wonder most is whether Jesus heard the hawkers. How piercing their words would have been: "Let's make a deal." "It costs you nothing." How easy it would have been for Jesus to have struck a bargain with Pilate! How easy it would have been to avoid having to pay the full price!

But Jesus didn't stop to haggle along the way. Unlike you and I, he didn't try to make a deal which would cost him nothing. Instead, fighting back the stench and sight of death before him, Jesus ignored the cries of the hawkers and hurried his weary steps to the cross.

There, on a precious hill far away, Jesus paid it all.

Jesus paid it all,
All to him I owe;
Sin had left a crimson stain,
He washed it white as snow.

—Elvina M. Hall

Chapter Thirty

"Besides him

there is no other."

DEUTERONOMY 4:35

Authority

For days I had driven around Mount Tabor on every side. From the tel at Megiddo I had looked across the Valley of Jezreel and seen its outline in the distance. From the Carmelite Monastery on Mount Carmel it had seemed but a hop, skip, and a jump to Tabor. Nazareth was only five miles away from the mountain, and the Sea of Galilee only ten. I'm not really sure why, but Mount Tabor kept beckoning to me from every direction.

I think what intrigued me most was the way it stood out on its own. It was not part of a chain of mountains or hills. It just rose abruptly some 1200 feet from the surrounding plain, looking much like a loaf of bread.

Had it not been for its association with biblical events, I might have given Tabor only passing notice. But I knew this particular mountain had been witness to mighty battles in the Valley of Jezreel; to Deborah and Barak, and Jabin, and Sisera. More importantly, I also knew that Mount Tabor was the probable setting for one of the most intriguing occurrences ever in the life of Jesus: His transfiguration.

So you can imagine my excitement as I approached Mount Tabor. While future visitors to the mount will undoubtedly find a well-paved road as they make their way up, I arrived when the road was under construction, making the already hazardous ascent even more of a challenge. Someone later told me there were thirty 180-degree hairpin switchbacks along the way, but I was too busy driving to count!

What I saw at the top was well worth the effort. The panoramic view from the summit is among the finest in all of Israel. Not only that, but I discovered a religious structure that has actually done justice to the site it was meant to commemorate. The Franciscan Church of the Transfiguration is simply lovely. It translates architecturally the tranquility of the gardenlike setting of Mount Tabor, and hints of the glory which must have accompanied the transfiguration.

I find it fascinating that when the psalmist referred to Mount Tabor, it was as if he were paving the way for the spectacular affirmation of Jesus' lordship that would one day take place on that very mountain. Look how the psalmist praises God for being preeminent among all the heavenly beings:

> *The heavens praise your wonders, O LORD,*
> *your faithfulness too, in the assembly of the holy ones.*
> *For who in the skies above can compare with the LORD?*
> *Who is like the LORD among the heavenly beings?*
> *In the council of the holy ones God is greatly feared;*
> *he is more awesome than all who surround him.*
>
> *O LORD God Almighty, who is like you?*
> *You are mighty, O LORD, and your faithfulness*
> *surrounds you. . . .*

The heavens are yours, and yours also the earth;
you founded the world and all that is in it.
You created the north and the south;
Tabor and Hermon sing for joy at your name.

Just as the psalmist said there was only one God, so there would be only one Lord and Savior of mankind. That's what the transfiguration of Jesus was all about: his preeminence. No wonder Tabor sang for joy!

Even the events immediately leading up to the extraordinary confirmation of Jesus' lordship seem to be consciously put there to set the scene. Remember when Jesus asked his disciples, "Who do people say the Son of Man is?" He wasn't just curious about rumors on the street. He was asking them the most important question you and I can ever ask: *Who is this man Jesus?*

But it was risky leaving the answer to public opinion, because public opinion was divided on the question. "Some say John the Baptist; others say Elijah; and still others, Jeremiah or one of the prophets." Even today, there are still risks. Hardly a month goes by without some newsstand magazine featuring an article by modern scholars who suggest that, instead of being truly divine, Jesus was simply an itinerant holy man who managed to gain a following far beyond his own expectations.

For such a crucial question—*Who is this man Jesus?*—public opinion is far too fickle; and skeptical religious scholarship is often woefully out of touch.

Nor is man's sense of timing a good indicator of spiritual authority. Many false messiahs before Jesus had "announced" the coming of the kingdom, and many would come after him (even today!) saying that the kingdom is yet to come. But Jesus knew that the actual appearance of the kingdom would be one of the surest confirmations of his lordship. No, not the *political* kingdom that so many, past and present, have envisioned, but the *spiritual* kingdom of a spiritual Messiah.

So in the very week prior to his transfiguration, Jesus said to his disciples, "I tell you the truth, some who are standing here will not taste death before they see the kingdom of God come with power." What excitement that must have caused, even for those who had misguided notions about the nature of the kingdom! What it meant was that the kingdom would come within their lifetime, in the generation that was living when Jesus walked the earth.

What it also meant was that, with the coming of the kingdom, would come the King! The King of kings and Lord of lords!

But how could anyone *really* know that Jesus was Lord and King? How could anyone *really* be sure?

Oddly, even Jesus' miracles would not be enough. The skeptics, of course, had prodded Jesus to demonstrate his divine status by performing miracles. For example, when Jesus routed the corrupt moneychangers in the temple, the Jewish leaders demanded, "What miraculous sign can you show us to prove your authority to do all this?"

At that moment in time they could hardly have believed that Jesus would ultimately demonstrate his preeminence by being resurrected from the dead. In the meantime, not even Jesus' miracles in giving sight to the blind and making the lame to walk were sufficiently convincing to the skeptical. After all, hadn't Moses performed miracles in Egypt and in the wilderness? Hadn't the prophet Elijah multiplied the widow's meal and raised her son from the dead? Hadn't he parted the waters of the Jordan with his cloak?

Over the centuries God had worked countless miracles through those whom he had called to serve as prophets. What reason did the Jews in Jesus' day have for thinking that, among all those holy men, Jesus was preeminent? Indeed, what reason did Jesus' own disciples have? As good Jews, they would have honored Jesus in much the same way as they did Moses and Elijah—as a great man of God. As a miracle worker. As a prophet whose message was worthy of reception.

But Jesus' preeminence, messiahship, lordship, ultimate authority—and, indeed, divinity—were yet to be demonstrated. And so we find Jesus taking Peter, James, and John and leading them "up a high mountain by themselves." (If indeed it was Mount Tabor, the climb from the bottom could have been made on foot in about an hour.) At the top, the disciples were apparently taking a rest while Jesus was praying. Suddenly Jesus' face was seen to shine like the sun! The apostles would later describe Jesus' clothes as "dazzling white, whiter than anyone in the world could bleach them." Or "as bright as a flash of lightning!"

Then—amazement of all amazements—the three apostles saw Moses and Elijah standing there with Jesus, talking about the events which would take place in Jerusalem when he would depart from the earth.

Of course, one could dismiss all of this as nothing more than a grandiose story made up by Jesus' disciples after his death. But if you believe, as I do, that it really happened just as they told it, then you simply have to stand in awe of this incredible event.

Just think, for example, of its implications for the afterlife. If Moses and Elijah were really there, then our spirits *really do* live beyond the grave!

Moreover, there must have been a power of recognition whereby it was possible for Jesus (and even for the apostles) to know who Moses and Elijah were. Does this not suggest that on the other side "I shall know fully, even as I am fully known"—that you and I will be able to instantly recognize Moses and Elijah as if we had known them all our lives? And perhaps our great-great-grandparents, whom we've never seen? The mind boggles!

Even *Peter's* mind boggled! Before he knew what he was doing, the always-impetuous Peter said to Jesus, "Master, it is good for us to be here. Let us put up three shelters—one for you, one for Moses and one for Elijah." Naturally, Peter thought he was doing the right thing by honoring all three.

But as if on cue, "a bright cloud enveloped them, and a voice from the cloud said, 'This is my Son, whom I love; with him I am well pleased. Listen to him!'" At that the disciples fell on their faces, terrified; and when they got up, Moses and Elijah had disappeared.

The point of the exercise could not have been missed: No matter what great servants Moses and Elijah had been, they were not to be viewed as the preeminent Lord and Savior of mankind. They were not the Son of God. They were not the Messiah. They were not the final authority in all things religious. They were not the King of kings and Lord of lords.

What God said of his Son that day on the summit of Mount Tabor was not just a repetition of what he had said on the occasion of Jesus' baptism: "This is my Son, whom I love; with him I am well pleased." It's those three additional words—*"Listen to him!"*—that tell the tale.

I stood there on the top of Mount Tabor, trying to imagine the bright light, the cloud, Moses, Elijah, Jesus, and the three apostles—but, most of all, the voice. The voice from heaven. The voice of God. The thundering, awesome, terrifying voice of Jehovah saying, *"Listen to him!"*

Or was it simply the "still small voice" of God that called to mind the personal struggle I have with giving the Lord complete preeminence in my life—that reminded me of my constant urge to look elsewhere for spiritual authority?

In some way every day I look to sources other than Jesus: to my parents and their faith. To a church I've grown up in. To the moral and ethical norms of a culture that couldn't care less about God. To peer pressure. To social expectations. Even (or especially) to my own logical mind and subjective experiences.

It is I who am enveloped in a cloud. It is I who have built a shelter to everyone and everything but Jesus. It is I who need to be facedown to the ground, terrified. Indeed, it is I who most need to be transfigured from without and transformed from within!

O Lord, hear my prayer. With each new day, speak to me out of the cloud. Let my face shine brighter and brighter with the light of your Son. And may my own story end just as theirs ended that glorious day on the mountain:

> *"When they looked up, they saw no one except Jesus."*

Chapter Thirty-one

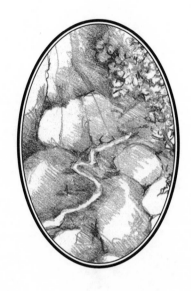

"God is my rock,

in whom I take refuge."

2 Samuel 22:3

Comfort

They are by no means the size of Mammoth Cave. Nor do they have anything inside them that begins to compare with the spectacular stalagmites and stalactites of Carlsbad Caverns. In fact, the Bell Caves are not caves at all, but only ancient quarries. Beautiful quarries. Cavelike quarries, except for the unusual amount of light which floods down through gaping holes at the top of each bell-shaped cavern and which also seeps in from yawning openings where walls from adjacent pits have caved in.

What takes you by surprise is that, from the ground above, you would never guess that a network of some 800 caves—many large enough to hold a ballistic missile upright—could possibly lie just beneath the surface. As you drive south from the ancient city of Maresha toward the newer city of Bet Guvrin—southwest of Jerusalem—all you see is typical Judean countryside. No scarred landscape. No huge, ugly hole in the ground so typical of quarries.

The Bell Caves were formed as a result of an unusual technique used in the quarrying process, itself made possible by the local geological structure of the region. In this area a hard, five-to-ten-foot-thick layer of crust (called nari) covers a soft chalky rock (called kirton) over 300 feet thick. Given that unique structure, the quarriers would begin by making a narrow hole in the crust and widening it as they dug deeper. The bell shape that resulted not only provided strong structural support but serendipitously preserved the moisture in the soft rock, protected the workers from the weather above ground, and gave easy access to the surface (by ropes) for both workers and stone blocks.

More important than the caves themselves is the story of their secondary use. The caves were dug in the seventh to tenth centuries after Christ by an Arabic-speaking Christian population. Throughout the caves are Arabic inscriptions, as well as drawings and crosses etched on the walls. Once the stones were removed, the people used the new underground caves for collecting water, for industrial use, for storage, for animal pens—even as burial sites and places of worship.

While visiting the Bell Caves, I was struck by the graceful beauty of the smooth, white-walled caverns; the serenity of their cool, quiet interiors; and the shafts of light penetrating what one would have expected to be an eerie darkness. Beauty. Serenity. Light. The caves were like an earthly heaven. Make that an *underground* heaven. In fact, make that an underground *haven*.

Heaven. Haven. What is heaven, anyway, if not an eternal haven? A place of peace and security. A place of rest. A place of comfort.

It seems to me that coming to know God is a lot like quarrying our way into such an idyllic place. We begin by penetrating the outer layer, which is the familiar world in which we live. On one hand, our world reveals the power and goodness of God. On the other hand, our world is like a hard crust that hides the spiritual world lying just beneath the surface. We have to dig to find the hidden treasure.

What I like about the Bell Caves is that the process of digging used by the workers was ecologically correct. They didn't just come in with a bunch of bulldozers and rape the land. They didn't leave scar tissue. They caused no ugliness. As if performing orthoscopic surgery, they left the landscape as it was, and yet penetrated deep within.

I think that is what God intends for us to do when we seek to know him—to be in the world, but not of it. To use his creation as a starting place. To take what we know from this world and use it to learn more about him. (Isn't that what Jesus' parables were all about?) Far from asking us to deny the world around us, or even leaving us to find him only in nature, God says to us, "Dig deep. True life is not just what you see around you, but a treasure I have hidden beneath the surface. Dig it up and bring it into your world. You can use it to build, to beautify, to glorify."

The irony is that the more deeply we dig into the heart of God in order to improve our lives in this world, the more otherworldly we become. If once a week, or once a day, or even once each hour we climb down from our world into his, we begin to see more and more of his love, his goodness, and his comfort.

God's heart is bell-shaped. The deeper we go, the wider it gets.

For an artist to properly depict the Bell Caves would take a canvas larger than any gallery could ever hold. How could one possibly paint on so grand a scale? Likewise, what can possibly compare with God's love? The apostle Paul could only begin to describe it when he prayed that we "may have power . . . to grasp how wide and long and high and deep is the love of Christ, and to know this love that surpasses knowledge—that you may be filled to the measure of all the fullness of God."

Who can experience such love without wanting to immerse oneself in it? Who can enter day after day into this otherworldly realm without one day realizing that what lies beneath the surface is more real than the material world in which we exist? Who can feel the comfort of God's secure spiritual haven without becoming uncomfortable with the world's ever-so-insecure alternative?

Unlike any cave I've ever explored, the deeper I go into the heart of God, the more light I see. Light for my pathway. Insight into God. Insight into my world. Insight into myself.

It must have been a great comfort to the young prophet Daniel when he and his fellow wise men were threatened with death in the palace of the Babylonian king. In the darkness of his troubled sleep, God sent a vision of insight which brought rescue and salvation. Daniel was overcome with sheer joy! "Praise be to the name of God for ever and ever; wisdom and power are his. . . . He reveals deep and hidden things; he knows what lies in darkness, and light dwells with him."

Who has ever sought comfort from God with more fervor and anguish than Job? When all around his world was crumbling, Job sought God in the depths of his own heart. Deeper and deeper he dug in search of answers. And the deeper he dug, the greater he appreciated God's love. The deeper he dug, the more he realized how little he could understand about God by merely standing on the surface looking down.

You can almost see Job at the bottom of his own bell-shaped quest for God—tethered to this cruel world by only a threadbare cord of defiant, trusting faith. Weary from the labor of quarrying God's awesome, elusive character, all that Job could do was to wipe his brow and praise his sovereign Creator. "To God belongs wisdom and power," said Job. "Counsel and understanding are his. . . . He reveals the deep things of darkness and brings deep shadows into the light."

Have you, like Job, ever stared down into darkness and found the light of God's wisdom hidden by your own shadow? Has sickness, or loneliness, or rejection made you long to be swallowed up in the depths of God's love? If so, the proverb is for you: "If you call out for insight and cry aloud for understanding, and if you look for it as for silver and search for it as for hidden treasure, then you will understand the fear of the LORD and find the knowledge of God. . . . For wisdom will enter your heart, and knowledge will be pleasant to your soul."

Search for God's comfort! *Dig deep* for it! Settle for nothing shallow. "I love those who love me," says God, "and those who seek me find me."

But with what shall we dig? How, by any means, can mortal man penetrate the crust of this material world to quarry the heart of God? The most amazing thing is that God reveals himself to those who make the effort to know him. If we must dig—if we must diligently and fervently search God's heart for the comfort we seek—nevertheless, God is like the "kirton"—*soft* rock, not hard like this world's own indifference to our greatest needs.

From the apostle Paul comes the wonderful assurance that "the Spirit searches all things, even the deep things of God. . . . We have not received the spirit of the world but the Spirit who is from

God, that we may understand what God has freely given us." Quarrying the heart of God is not like digging with a blunted shovel. It's more like being lowered into one of the Bell Caves on a rope and discovering blocks of stone which have already been hewn by somebody else.

The greatest comfort of all is knowing that we are not alone in our search for comfort.

In fact—as with the heart of God itself—the deeper we go into our own pit of hopelessness, loneliness, fear, or despair, the greater we experience God's love. If we usually tend to think of God being *up there* in heaven somewhere, rather than in the depths of some ancient quarry, even so, the truth is that there is no place where we cannot find God's love.

Like us, the psalmist looked heavenward in his adulation of God, saying, "Your righteousness reaches to the skies, O God, you who have done great things." But the psalmist could just as well have been at the bottom of a deep, dank quarry when he wrote, "Though you have made me see troubles, many and bitter, you will restore my life again; from the depths of the earth you will again bring me up. You will increase my honor and comfort me once again."

After all, when do we most need comforting? When we are on a mountaintop, or when we are in the pits? Without question, God knows full well when we need him most. How could we ever forget that our Savior himself was buried in a quarry? When Joseph of Arimathea had taken Jesus' body down from the cross, he wrapped it in linen cloth and placed it in a "tomb cut in the rock."

Had the story ended there, of course, there would be no comfort in Christ. The quarry of death would have held captive its prey, and the heart of God would not be deep enough or wide enough to care about what happens to the rest of us. But the psalmist's words have meaning for us precisely because they had meaning for Jesus: "From the depths of the earth you will again bring me up. You will increase my honor and comfort me once again."

By the ropes of his divine power, God lifted up "a stone in Zion, a tested stone, a precious cornerstone for a sure foundation" of his temple. By those same ropes of grace, God lifts us up from the bosom of his heart and gives us new life, new hope, new vision for what he has called us to be.

And this is where the picture of God's heart as a cavernous bell-shaped haven of comfort takes the most interesting turn of all. The prophet Isaiah changes the metaphor so that not just *Christ* is hewn out and lifted up as the chief cornerstone, but *we ourselves* become hewn from him who is the Rock of Ages. "Listen to me," says Isaiah, "you who pursue righteousness and who seek the LORD: Look to the rock from which you were cut and to the quarry from which you were hewn." Is there a greater expression of hope and expectancy? "The LORD will surely comfort Zion and will look with compassion on all her ruins; he will make her deserts like Eden, her wastelands like the garden of the LORD. Joy and gladness will be found in her, thanksgiving and the sound of singing."

Comfort. Compassion. Joy. Gladness. Thanksgiving. Singing. All from the depths of a heavenlike quarry. All from the immeasurable depth and breadth of the heart of an ineffable God.

There is a place of quiet rest,
Near to the heart of God;
A place where sin cannot molest,
Near to the heart of God.

There is a place of comfort sweet,
Near to the heart of God;
A place where we our Savior meet,
Near to the heart of God.

There is a place of full release,
Near to the heart of God;
A place where all is joy and peace,
Near to the heart of God.

O Jesus, blest Redeemer,
Sent from the heart of God,
Hold us, who wait before Thee,
Near to the heart of God.

—Cleland B. McAfee

SCRIPTURE REFERENCES

In Holy Places—
Matthew 23:37-39; 8:23-27; Mark 4:35-41; Luke 8:22-25; Matthew 14:28-33; Mark 6:51,52;
Matthew 17:1-8; Mark 9:2-8; Luke 9:28-36; Matthew 6:26; 1 Samuel 17:1-58.

1. Bethlehem—
Luke 2:1-20; 1 Samuel 16:1-12; Genesis 35:19; Matthew 2:1-12; Micah 5:2; Luke 1:26-38;
John 1:1,14.

2. The Holy Sepulcher—
John 20:29; Romans 6:3,4; 1 Kings 13:1-32; 2 Kings 23:16-18; Numbers 19:16; Ezekiel 37:1-14;
Matthew 26:30.

3. Valley of Gehenna—
2 Chronicles 33:6; 1 Kings 11:6,7; Jeremiah 7:31-33; 2 Kings 23:8-16; 2 Chronicles 34:1-5;
Mark 9:48; Matthew 5:29,30; 18:8,9; Mark 9:43-47; Luke 12:5; Matthew 13:49,50;
Matthew 10:28; Revelation 20:12-15; Genesis 22:1-14; Matthew 27:46,51.

4. The Wailing Wall—
Mark 13:1,2; Esther 4:1-3; 1 Kings 8:27; 2 Chronicles 6:18; Ezekiel 10:4; 43:5; 2 Chronicles
20:9; Jonah 2:7; Micah 3:12; Amos 8:3; 2 Kings 24:20; Nehemiah 4:1,2; John 2:19-21;
1 Corinthians 3:16,17; Psalm 30:11.

5. The Dead Sea—
Deuteronomy 32:48-52; Numbers 27:12-14; Genesis 13:5-12; Genesis 18:22-33; 19:1-28;
Matthew 5:22; 10:28; 18:9; 23:15; 23:33; Luke 17:28,29; Deuteronomy 29:23; 29:19;
Ezekiel 16:49,50; Luke 17:32,33.

6. The Ossuary—
Matthew 26:13; Luke 10:38-42; John 11:1-4; 11:17-45; 12:1-8; Matthew 26:6-13; Mark 14:3-9;
Romans 2:28,29; 1 Peter 3:3,4; 2 Corinthians 5:12; Matthew 26:28; Mark 14:24; Luke 22:20;
1 Samuel 16;7; Romans 5:5; Philippians 2:7; Titus 3:4-7.

7. David's Wadi—
Song of Songs 1:14; 6:13; 1 Kings 1:1-4; 1 Samuel 23:29; 24:1-7; Psalm 42:4; 1 Samuel 18:5-11;
Psalm 42:1,3,5,6,7,8.

8. Pool of Bethesda—
John 5:1-47; Matthew 12:9-14; Mark 3:1-6; Luke 6:6-11; Matthew 12:1-8; Mark 2:23-28;
Luke 6:1-5; John 5:17.

9. Model of Second Temple—
Ephesians 2:14; Acts 21:27—22:29; Matthew 7:24-27; Hebrews 11:10; Revelation 21:21.

10. Qumran—
Acts 2:38; Matthew 3:1-10; Mark 1:2-6; Luke 3:1-14; Hebrews 10:22; Philippians 4:8.

11. The Tels—
Mark 1:21-28; Matthew 11:20-23; Matthew 8:5-13; Luke 7:1-10; Matthew 8:14,15;
Mark 1:29-31; Acts 16:1; 2 Timothy 1:5; Ephesians 2:20; 1 Corinthians 3:9-11; Job 8:8-10.

12. The Good Fence—
Joshua 22:25; Job 26:10; Jeremiah 5:22; Proverbs 8:29; Deuteronomy 19:14; 27:17; Psalm 16:6;
Ephesians 2:14.

13. The Bedouins—
Luke 10:25-37; Jeremiah 8:7; 1 Kings 10:1-13; 2 Chronicles 9:1-12; Matthew 2:1-16;
Genesis 4:12; Genesis 47:9; Hebrews 11:13-16; Jeremiah 50:6; 1 Peter 1:1,17; Genesis 12:1.

14. Masada—
Romans 5:7,8; John 15:13; 1 John 3:16; Philippians 1:20; Ecclesiastes 9:4.

15. Pool of Siloam—
2 Chronicles 32:2-4; 2 Kings 20:20; John 9:1—10:21.

16. Megiddo—
Judges 4:1-24; 2 Kings 9:1-27; 2 Chronicles 35:20-24; 2 Kings 23:29,30; 1 Kings 9:15;
1 Corinthians 15:33; 1 Peter 2:11; Romans 7:23; 1 Chronicles 5:20; Psalm 69:19; 13:2; 60:12;
Revelation 14:14—16:21; John 19:30; Psalm 23:5.

17. Mount Carmel—
1 Kings 17:1; 17:2-7; 17:8-16; 17:17-24; 19:1-18; 16:32,33; 18:20-40; 2 Timothy 1:12;
Ephesians 4:14; James 4:8; Matthew 6:24; Luke 16:13; Colossians 3:5.

18. The Broad Wall—
2 Chronicles 32:2-5; 2 Kings 25:2-6; Jeremiah 39:2-5; Nehemiah 1:1—2:18; 3:1-32;
Isaiah 58:6,7,12.

19. The Gaza Road—
Luke 1:5-25; 57-80; Judges 13:2-25; 2 Kings 18:13-37; Isaiah 36:1-22; 1 Samuel 17:1-58;
Acts 8:26; Acts 8:36; Luke 23:46.

20. Passover—
Exodus 12:25-27; Joshua 4:6,7; Psalm 78:1-6; Proverbs 13:22; Joel 1:3.

21. Gethsemane—
Luke 22:39; John 18:3; Matthew 26:30-35; Mark 14:26-31; Matthew 26:36-46; Mark 14:32-41;
Luke 22:40-46; 2 Samuel 15:30; Psalm 3; Matthew 21:9; Deuteronomy 21:18-21;
Hebrews 5:7-9; 2 Samuel 18:33.

22. Mount of Olives—
Acts 1:6-11; Matthew 24:36; Mark 16:19; Luke 24:50-52; 2 Kings 2:1-11.

23. The Judean Desert—
Matthew 4:1-11; Mark 1:12,13; Luke 4:1-13; Matthew 3:17; Proverbs 16:18; Hebrews 4:15; Ephesians 4:26; 1 Corinthians 10:13; James 1:14,15.

24. Via Dolorosa—
John 19:5 KJV; Matthew 27:32; Mark 15:21; Luke 23:26,28; Matthew 16:24; Mark 8:34; Luke 9:23; 14:27; 1 Chronicles 21:24; Luke 19:41-44; Isaiah 53:3.

25. Sea of Galilee—
Luke 5:4-11; Matthew 8:23-27; Mark 4:35-41; Luke 8:22-25; Matthew 14:22-34; Mark 6:45-53; John 6:16-21; Matthew 16:13-19.

26. Jordan River—
Matthew 3:5,6; Mark 1:4,5; Luke 3:1-3; John 1:24-28; Matthew 3:13-17; Mark 1:9-11; Luke 3:21,22; Genesis 32:10; 2 Kings 2:1-15; Matthew 3:16; Acts 2:38; 2 Kings 5:1-14; Joshua 3:7—4:18; Exodus 3:8; Numbers 13:27.

27. Mount of Beatitudes—
Matthew 5:1—7:29; Luke 6:30,31; Jeremiah 10:23; Matthew 6:25-34; 5:21,22; 7:22,23; 1 Samuel 16:7; Matthew 7:1,16; 5:16; 6:1.

28. Dome of the Rock—
1 Chronicles 22:1; Exodus 3:1-6; 1 Timothy 2:8; Psalm 5:7; 72:11; 95:6; Exodus 20:5; 23:24; Leviticus 26:1; Isaiah 2:8; Joshua 5:13-15; Matthew 4:9,10; 16:16-18; Philippians 2:9-11; Hebrews 12:22-29.

29. The Souk—
Genesis 23:3-20; 18:16-33; Matthew 8:21,22; Luke 9:59-62; 1 Chronicles 21:18-25; John 19:31; 18:28; Luke 22:15.

30. Mount Tabor—
Psalm 89:5-12; Matthew 16:13-20; Mark 8:27-30; Luke 9:18-20; Mark 9:1; Matthew 16:28; Luke 9:27; John 2:18; Matthew 17:1-8; Mark 9:2-8; Luke 9:28-36; 1 Corinthians 13:12; Matthew 3:17; Mark 1:11; Luke 3:22.

31. The Bell Caves—
Ephesians 3:18,19; Daniel 2:20,22; Job 12:13,22; Proverbs 2:3-5,10; 8:17; 1 Corinthians 2:10,12; Psalm 71:19-21; Luke 23:53; Isaiah 28:16; 51:1,3.